JAVASCRIPT

Quick Reference

JavaScript

Quick Reference

Rick Darnell

que®

Credits

President
Roland Elgey

Publisher
Joseph B. Wikert

Publishing Manager
Fred Slone

Senior Title Manager
Bryan Gambrel

Editorial Services Director
Elizabeth Keaffaber

Managing Editor
Sandy Doell

Acquisitions Editor
Angela C. Kozlowski

Production Editor
Mike La Bonne

Editor
Judith Goode

Strategic Marketing Manager
Barry Pruett

Product Marketing Manager
Kim Margolius

Assistant Product Marketing Manager
Christy M. Miller

Technical Editor
Steven Tallon

Technical Support Specialist
Nadeem Muhammed

Acquisitions Coordinator
Bethany A. Echlin

Software Relations Coordinator
Patty Brooks

Editorial Assistant
Andrea Duvall

Book Designer
Nathan Clement

Cover Designer
Nathan Clement

Production Team
Marcia Brizendine
Jenny Earhart
DiMonique Ford
Amy Gornik
Michelle Lee
Kaylene Riemen

Indexer
Tim Tate

Composed in Frutiger and ITC Kabel by Que Corporation.

To Jane, Margaret, and Elizabeth

About the Author

Rick Darnell is a freelance writer and dad who has been working with computers since the early days of the personal computer, beginning with a Radio Shack Model I. He's contributed to several titles for Que, including *Using JavaScript*, *Intranet Toolkit*, *Internet Expert Solutions*, *Running a Perfect Web Site for Windows*, and *Using PowerPoint for Windows 95*. Rick has worked as a journalist for newspapers in Kansas and Wyoming, and as a contributing author for various trade and literary publications. In his spare time, Rick is a firefighter with the Missoula Rural Fire District, where he is also a member of a regional hazardous materials response team.

Acknowledgments

A very heartfelt thank you to Lisa Wagner and the folks at Que who were willing to give an unknown a chance to try his hand at book writing. This includes special thanks to Doshia Stewart, who for some unknown reason kept calling with project ideas until we found a match—her patience and support are invaluable.

My editor on this project, Angela Kozlowski, gets the award for patience and tenacity. She gave me the chance to work on this project and ended up competing for my attention with the biggest chlorine spill in the history of the northwest region. It takes an editor with a strong stomach to work with an author that smells like bleach for two weeks.

Finally, I would be terribly remiss not to acknowledge the people who have given me valuable advice and direction at crucial points in my writing career—David MacFarland, Larry Walker, and John Braden. Your influence is always present.

We'd Like to Hear from You!

As part of our continuing effort to produce books of the highest possible quality, Que would like to hear your comments. To stay competitive, we *really* want you, as a computer book reader and user, to let us know what you like or dislike most about this book or other Que products.

You can mail comments, ideas, or suggestions for improving future editions to the address below, or send us a fax at (317) 581-4663. For the online inclined, Macmillan Computer Publishing has a forum on CompuServe (type **GO QUEBOOKS** at any prompt) through which our staff and authors are available for questions and comments. The address of our Internet site is **http://www.mcp.com** (World Wide Web).

In addition to exploring our forum, please feel free to contact me personally to discuss your opinions of this book: I'm Angela C. Kozlowski at CompuServe 75703,3504, and akozlowski@que.mcp.com on the Internet.

Thanks in advance--your comments will help us to continue publishing the best books available on computer topics in today's market.

Angela C. Kozlowski
Acquisitions Editor
Que Corporation
201 W. 103rd Street
Indianapolis, Indiana 46290
USA

Contents at a Glance

Table of Contents

JavaScript Quick Reference

Contents

JavaScript Quick Reference

JavaScript Quick Reference

xxi

Contents

JavaScript Quick Reference

JavaScript Quick Reference

INTRODUCTION

JavaScript is a scripting language used with HTML pages to increase functionality and interaction with the end user. It was developed by Netscape with Sun's Java language.

Finding information on programming in JavaScript can be a bit like looking for the Holy Grail. Among Netscape's site, online tutorials, and examples, information seems to be everywhere but at your fingertips. So here is the information you're looking for in one place, including statements, operators, and color values.

JavaScript and Java

It's important to note that JavaScript is a completely different beast from Java. Java is an object-oriented programming language developed by Sun Microsystems, and needs a variety of compilers and support files to function. It is useful for programmers and developers who have prior programming experience with languages like C++.

Programs developed under the Java development kit can work as full-fledged, stand-alone applications or as *applets* embedded in HTML pages. Even though applets are embedded in HTML pages, they still arrive on the client's computer as separate files.

JavaScript was developed by Netscape. It is a cousin to Java, containing a smaller and simpler set of commands that vary slightly in their implementation.

JavaScript's structure and syntax are similar to Java's but JavaScript is only functional when included as part of an HTML page. You can't develop applets or stand-alone applications with JavaScript—it can only reside within an HTML script and function when loaded on a compatible browser such as Netscape 2.0.

Using This Book

Several conventions used in this book make finding information easier.

Each entry has the same basic structure. Following the term and its type (object, property, or method) is a brief description of its use. This is followed by the syntax of the command.

Some items, especially those relating to forms, have a variety of implementations. The basic variations are listed as part of the syntax. *Italicized* items need to be replaced with actual values or variable names. Given the following syntax:

document.*formName*

a form called `userInfo` would be implemented this way:

```
document.userInfo
```

Methods with an asterisk are built-in methods and don't need association with an object to function.

A detailed description of use and programming examples is next, followed by a cross-reference to related items in the book.

When you see the term URL, it refers to a complete universal resource locator, including type and machine address, plus path and hash if applicable.

General Terms

Although they are not necessarily JavaScript objects or keywords, the following terms can help you understand JavaScript and how it works. These include general terms used in most discussions about JavaScript and its implementation.

Event Handlers

Event handlers are a special item in JavaScript and give it much of its power. They allow the programmer to look for specific user behavior in relation to the HTML page, such as clicking a form button or moving the mouse pointer over an anchor.

Event handlers are embedded in HTML tags, typically used as part of forms, but are also included as a part of some anchors and links.

Virtually anything a user can do to interact with a page is covered with the event handlers, from moving the mouse to leaving the current page. For example, the following line displays "Netscape's Home Page" in the status bar instead of the link's URL when the mouse is placed over the anchor.

```
<A HREF="home.netscape.com"
onMouseOver="window.status='Netscape's Home Page';
return true">
```

Functions

A function is a user-defined or built-in method that performs a task. It can also return a value when used with the `return` statement. Functions are universal and do not need to be associated with an object to run, while methods are integrated with objects.

As a general rule, it's best to place function definitions within the `<HEAD>` tags of a document. This practice ensures that any functions are loaded and ready before the user has a chance to interact with the rest of the page.

Hierarchies

In a hierarchy, objects exist in a set relation to each other. For example, Navigator objects have a structure that reflects the construction of an HTML page. This is called *instance hierarchy* because it only works with specific instances of objects rather than with general classes.

The `window` object is the parent of all other Navigator objects. Underneath the `window` object, `location`, `history`, and `document` all share precedence. Under `document` are other objects such as forms, links, and anchors.

Each object is a descendant of a higher object. A form called `orderForm` is an object and it is also a property of `document`. As such, it is called `document.orderForm`.

Another way to think about a hierarchy is the relationship items in the real world have to each other. Spokes, handlebars, and pedals are all objects that belong to a bicycle. A bicycle is an object that belongs to ground transportation. Ground transportation is an object that belongs to modes of travel.

If represented as JavaScript objects, these relationships could be expressed this way:

```
travelMode.groundTransport.bicycle.handleBars
```

The highest and most nonspecific object is on the left and it gains specificity as it moves to the right and its descendants begin to branch out.

Java

In the words of Sun Microsystems, "Java is a simple, robust, object-oriented, platform-independent, multithreaded, dynamic, general-purpose programming environment." What all these buzz-words mean is that Java is ideally suited for creating applets and applications for the Internet, for intranets, and for any other complex, distributed network.

Once compiled, it is possible for a single piece of Java source code to run on any machine—Windows 95, Solaris, Macintosh, or any other—that is equipped with a Java interpreter. Programming in Java requires a Java Development Kit with compiler and core classes provided by Sun or a third-party vendor, such as Symantec.

JavaScript

JavaScript is a scripting language for HTML documents developed by Netscape in cooperation with Sun Microsystems. Scripts are performed after specific user-triggered events. Creating JavaScript Web documents requires a text editor and compatible browser. Netscape Gold also includes an editor within the browser itself, so an external text editor isn't necessary.

Although not directly related to Java, JavaScript can interact with the exposed properties and methods of Java applets embedded on an HTML page. The difference boils down to this—Java applets exist outside the browser, whereas JavaScript exists only within a browser.

Literals

A literal is a value that can be assigned to a variable. Literals are what they are and do not change. Examples include 1, 3.1415927, "Bob," and `true`.

Several types of literals in JavaScript correspond to the variable types.

Integers

Integers are whole numbers such as 1, 16, and 25,896. They can be expressed in decimal (base 10), hexadecimal (base 16), or octal (base 8) form.

Hexadecimal numbers include 0–9 and a–f, and are represented in Java-Script by preceding the number with 0x (zero–x). Octal numbers only include 0–7 and are preceded by 0 (zero).

For example, decimal 23 is represented in hexadecimal by 0x17 and in octal by 027.

Floating-Point Numbers

Floating-point numbers are fractional portions of integers and must include at least one digit, and a decimal point or exponent symbol ("e" or "E").

The following are all ways of expressing the same floating-point number:

```
3.1415927
3145927e-7
.3141527E1
```

Boolean Literals

Boolean literals have only two values, true or false. In some implementations of JavaScript, 0 (false) and 1 (true) cannot be substituted for Boolean values. The current versions of Netscape Navigator and Gold both support 0 and 1 as Boolean false and true.

Strings

Strings are defined by any number of characters within single or double quotation marks. Using the backslash "\" can escape the quotation marks to print special characters.

```
document.write("Doc said, \"Festus, you need a
bath,\" and wrinkled his nose.")
```

results in

```
Doc said, "Festus, you need a bath," and wrinkled
his nose.
```

Methods

A method is a function assigned to an object. For example,
`userName.toUpperCase()` returns an uppercase version of the
string contained in `userName`.

Objects

An object is a construct with properties that are JavaScript variables or
other objects. Functions associated with an object are called the
object's methods. You access the properties and methods of an object
with a simple notation:

```
objectName.propertyName
objectName.methodName
```

All names are case-sensitive.

If an object called `house` has the properties of `bedrooms`, `bath-
rooms`, `floors`, and `squareFeet`, you could access its values by us-
ing the object notation:

```
house.bedrooms
house.bathrooms
house.floors
house.squareFeet
```

Another way of thinking of objects is an array using the following array
notation:

```
house["bedrooms"]
house["bathrooms"]
house["floors"]
house["squareFeet"]
```

The same object is also represented in JavaScript by a traditional array:

```
house[0]
house[1]
house[2]
house[3]
```

This type of relationship between indexes and strings is called an *associative array*.

Creating a new object requires a function that *instantiates* (creates an *instance* of) the object. Using the house example, the following function would create a new instance of a `house` object:

```
function House(bedrooms, bathrooms, floors,
squareFeet) {
    this.bedrooms = bedrooms;
    this.bathrooms = bathrooms;
    this.floors = floors;
    this.squareFeet = squareFeet
}
```

Now that the object is defined, an instance is created by using the `new` directive:

```
500South5th = new House(2, 1, 1, 1700)
```

Other objects can be included as part of the object definition. For example, an object called `owner` has properties called `name`, `age`, `mortgageLength`.

```
function Owner(name, age, mortgageLength) {
    this.name = name;
    this.age = age;
    this.mortgageLength = mortgageLength
}
```

Adding an additional argument and line to the `House` function adds an owner to the house:

```
function House(bedrooms, bathrooms, floors,
squareFeet, owner) {
    this.bedrooms = bedrooms;
    this.bathrooms = bathrooms;
    this.floors = floors;
```

```
      this.squareFeet = squareFeet;
      this.owner = owner
}
```

Now owner Glenn Woodson, 38, with a 20-year mortgage, represented by G_Woodson is included with the house:

```
G_Woodson = new Owner("Glenn Woodson",38,20);
500South5th = new House(2, 1, 1, 1700, G_Woodson)
```

The properties of G_Woodson are included as part of 500South5th:

```
500South5th.bedrooms
500South5th.bathrooms
500South5th.floors
500South5th.squareFeet
500South5th.G_Woodson.name
500South5th.G_Woodson.age
500South5th.G_Woodson.mortgageLength
```

Operators

An operator performs a function on one or more operands or variables. Operators are divided into two basic classes: binary and unary. Binary operators need two operands and unary operators need a single operand.

For example, addition is a binary operand:

```
sum = 1 + 5
```

Unary operands are often used to update counters. The following example increases the counter variable by 1:

```
counter++
```

Properties

Properties are used to describe an object or its current state. A property is defined by assigning it a value. The value can be assigned by the browser, the program, or as the user interacts with the page.

Several properties in JavaScript contain *constants*—values that never change. These are items such as the value of Pi or Euler's constant (E). Other items change from page to page but can't be changed, such as form elements.

Scripts

One or more JavaScript commands can be enclosed in a `<SCRIPT>` tag. The advent of several scripting languages has made it necessary to identify for the browser which language is being used. For JavaScript, the syntax is:

```
<SCRIPT LANGUAGE="JavaScript">
<!--
...Statements...
// -->
</SCRIPT>
```

The use of the LANGUAGE attribute is still optional in Netscape browsers, but this could change if other languages, such as Microsoft's VBScript, are implemented.

Note the use of HTML comment tags, `<!--` and `-->`. If the page containing the script is used on a browser that is not compatible with the scripting languages, the script statements are displayed as any other text on the page, adding clutter and trash to the screen.

If you use the comment tags, an incompatible browser ignores the script portion of the document. The double slashes that precede the closing HTML comment tag ensure that the tag won't be mistaken for a JavaScript statement.

Type Casting

A variable's type depends on the kind of information it contains (see "Literals"). JavaScript is loosely typed, meaning it does not need variables to declare what kind of type they are when created. The type is automatically assigned depending on the literal assigned to the variable.

Type Casting

By the same token, the type can change depending on the operation. Take the following statements:

```
//example 1
var oneString = "1"
var oneInt = 1
var oneConcatenate = oneString + oneInt //Results
in "11"
var oneAddition = oneInt + oneString //Results in 2
```

In the first addition statement, the first operator is a string. JavaScript assumes that the operation is to join two strings. When JavaScript encounters an integer in the second operator, it converts the variable to a string to meet its own expectations.

Since JavaScript does not maintain any methods or properties to determine the current type for a variable, it is important to monitor the use of variables closely to avoid unexpected results.

REFERENCE

J avaScript syntax and commands are divided into several categories depending on their use and function.

Objects are the building blocks of JavaScript. They are used to return and modify the status of forms, pages, the browser, and programmer-defined variables. An easy way to think about an object is as a noun. Cat, car, house, computer, and form are all nouns and could all be represented as an object (see "Objects").

We use *properties* to differentiate between objects of the same class—for example, all objects that are a cat. Properties are adjectives and refer to items that might make the object different from other objects. In the cat example, this could be weight, color, breed, disposition, and current activity (see "Properties").

We use *methods* to pass messages to the object and sometimes to change its properties. For example, one method could be used to change the cat's current activity from eating to sleeping, whereas another could be used to change its weight from heavy to really heavy (see "Methods").

Following is a listing of the building blocks of JavaScript:

abs

(Method)

Returns the absolute (unsigned) value of its argument.

```
Math.abs(argument)
```

Usage

The following example returns 10 and 12.5, respectively.

```
document.writeln(Math.abs(-10));
John.age.value = 12.5
document.writeln(Math.abs(John.age.value))
```

Related Items

Method of `Math`.

acos

(Method)

Returns the arc cosine (from 0 to π radians) of its argument.

```
Math.acos(argument)
```

Usage

The argument should be a number between –1 and 1. If the value is outside the valid range, a 0 is returned.

Related Items

Method of `Math`.

See the `asin`, `atan`, `cos`, `sin`, and `tan` methods.

action

(Property)

A reflection of the action attribute in an HTML <FORM> tag.

```
document.formName.action
document.forms[index].action
```

Usage

`action` returns a string consisting of a destination URL for data submitted from a form. This value can be set or changed before or after the document has been loaded and formatted.

In this example, the `action` for a form called `outlineForm` is set to the URL in the variable `outlineURL`.

```
outlineURL = "http://www.wossamottau.edu/cgi-bin/
➥outline.cgi"
outlineForm.action=outlineURL
```

Related Items

Property of `form`.

See the `encoding`, `method`, and `target` properties.

alert

(Method)

Displays a JavaScript Alert dialog box with an OK button and a user-defined message (see fig. QR.1).

```
[window.]alert(AlertMessage)
```

Fig. QR.1 Users must click the OK button in a JavaScript alert box before they can return to the document.

Usage

Before users can continue with an operation, they must press the OK button in the alert box.

Related Items

Method of `window`.

See the `confirm` and `prompt` methods.

alinkColor

(Property)

The color of a link after the mouse button is pressed but before it's released.

```
document.alinkColor
```

Usage

Like all colors in JavaScript, alinkColor is expressed as a hexadecimal RGB triplet or string literal. It cannot be changed after the HTML source document is processed. Both of these examples set the color to alice blue.

```
document.alinkColor="aliceblue"
document.alinkColor="F0F8FF"
```

Related Items

Property of `document`.

See the `bgColor`, `fgColor`, `linkColor`, and `vlinkColor` properties.

anchor

(Method)

Creates and displays an HTML hypertext target.

```
textString.anchor(anchorName)
```

Usage

Used with `write` or `writeln` methods, `anchor` creates an HTML anchor in the current document, where `textString` is what the user sees and `anchorName` is equivalent to the `name` attribute of an HTML `<ANCHOR>` tag.

```
anchorString = "Louie's Place";
document.writeln(anchorString.anchor("louies_place")
```

Related Items

Method of `string`.

See the `link` method.

anchors

(Property)

An array of all defined anchors in the current document. See the `anchor` object for a detailed description.

```
document.anchors[index]
```

Usage

If the length of an anchor array in a document is 5, then the `anchors` array is represented as `document.anchors[0]` through `document.anchors[4]`.

Related Items

Property of `document`.

See the `anchor` object.

See the `length` and `links` properties.

anchors array

(Object)

An array containing information about possible targets of a hypertext link in a document.

`[windowName.]document.anchors[index]`

Usage

`anchors array` is a read-only object that is set in HTML with `<A>` tags.

```
<A [HREF=URL] NAME="anchor name"
[TARGET="windowName"]>
anchor text
</A>
```

Including a value for `HREF` also makes the anchor a link and adds it to the `links` array. New anchors are defined with JavaScript by using the `anchor` method.

To determine how many anchors are included in a document, use the `length` property.

`document.anchors.length`

The value of `document.anchor[index]` returns null. For example, the value of `document.anchor[0]` returns `null` even though it was the first anchor created with `<A NAME="bob">All about Bob</` ➡`A>`.

Related Items

Property of `document`.

See the `link` object and the `anchor` method.

appCodeName

(Property)

Returns a read-only string with the code name of the browser.

`navigator.appCodeName`

Usage

To display the code name for the current browser, use the following line:

```
document.write("The code name of your browser is "
➥+ navigator.appCodeName + ".")
```

For Netscape Navigator 2.0, this returns:

```
The name of your browser is Mozilla.
```

Related Items

Property of `navigator`.

See the `appName`, `appVersion`, and `userAgent` properties.

appName

(Property)

Returns a read-only string with the name of the browser.

```
navigator.appName
```

Usage

To display the application name for the current browser, use the following line:

```
document.write("The name of your browser is " +
➥navigator.appName + ".")
```

For Netscape Navigator 2.0, this returns:

```
The code name of your browser is Netscape.
```

Related Items

Property of `navigator`.

See the `appCodeName`, `appVersion`, and `userAgent` properties.

appVersion

(Property)

Returns a string with the browser version information.

```
navigator.appVersion
```

Usage

`appVersion` is used to check which browser version the client is using. It returns in the *releaseNumber (platform; country)* format. For a Windows 95 release of Netscape 2.0:

```
document.write("The version of your browser is: " +
➥navigator.appVersion + ".")
```

returns

```
The version of your browser is: 2.0 (Win95; I).
```

This specifies an international release of Navigator 2.0 running on Windows 95. The U country code specifies a U.S. release, whereas an I indicates an international release.

Related Items

Property of `navigator`.

See the `appName`, `appCodeName`, and `userAgent` properties.

asin

(Method)

Returns the arc sine of its argument.

```
Math.asin(argument)
```

Usage

Passing a number between −1 and 1 to `asin` returns the arcsine (between $-\pi/2$ and $\pi/2$ radians). If the number is outside the range, a 0 is returned.

Related Items

Method of `Math`.

See the `acos`, `atan`, `cos`, `sin`, and `tan` methods.

atan

(Method)

Returns the arc tangent of its argument.

```
Math.(argument)
```

Usage

`atan` returns a number between –Π/2 and Π/2 radians, representing the size of an angle in radians. Its argument is a number between –1 and 1, representing the tangent.

Related Items

Method of `Math`.

See the `acos`, `asin`, `cos`, `sin`, and `tan` methods.

back

(Method)

Recalls the previous URL from the history list.

```
history.back()
```

Usage

The usage for `back` is the same as for `history.go(-1)`.

Related Items

Method of `history`.

See the `forward` and `go` methods.

bgColor

(Property)

The document background color.

```
document.bgColor
```

Usage

The usage for bgColor overrides the background color set in the browser preferences. It is expressed as a hexadecimal RGB triplet or string literal. It can be changed at any time. The following example allows users to use radio buttons to set their own background color.

```
function newColor(colorString) {
    document.bgColor = colorString
}
...
<FORM NAME="colors">
<INPUT TYPE="radio" NAME="color" VALUE="F0F8FF"
➥onClick="newColor(this.value)">Alice Blue
<INPUT TYPE="radio" NAME="color" VALUE="FF4500"
➥onClick="newColor(this.value)">Ochre
<INPUT TYPE="radio" NAME="color" VALUE="FFEFD5"
➥onClick="newColor(this.value)">Papaya Whip
</FORM>
```

Related Items

Property of document.

See the alinkColor, fgColor, linkColor, and vlinkColor properties.

big

(Method)

Formats a string object as a big font.

```
stringName.big()
```

Usage

Functionally, the usage for `big` is the same as encasing text with HTML `<BIG>` tags. Both of the following examples result in the same output: displaying the message "Welcome to my home page" in a big font:

```
var welcomeMessage = "Welcome to my home page."
document.write(welcomeMessage.big())
```

```
<BIG> Welcome to my home page.</BIG>
```

Related Items

Method of `string`.

See the `fontsize` and `small` methods.

blink

(Method)

Formats a `string` object as a blinking line.

```
stringname.blink()
```

Usage

The usage for `blink` same as encasing text with HTML `<BLINK>` tags. Both of the following examples produce a flashing line that says, "Notice":

```
var attentionMessage = "Notice"
document.write(attentionMessage.blink())
```

```
<BLINK>Notice</BLINK>
```

Related Items

Method of `string`.

See the `bold`, `italics`, and `strike` methods.

blur

(Method)

Removes focus from the specified `form` element.

```
document.formName.elementName.blur()
document.forms[index].elements[index].blur()
```

Usage

For example, the following line removes focus from the `feedback` element:

```
feedback.blur()
```

assuming that `feedback` is defined as:

```
<INPUT TYPE="text" NAME="feedback">
```

Related Items

Method of `password`, `select`, `text`, and `textarea`.

See the `focus` and `select` methods.

bold

(Method)

Formats a `string` object in bold text.

```
stringName.bold()
```

Usage

The usage for `bold` is the same as encasing text with HTML `<B>` tags.

Related Items

Method of `string`.

See the `blink`, `italics`, and `strike` methods.

button

(Object)

A pushbutton on a form.

```
formName.buttonName
forms[index].elements[index]
```

Usage

Buttons must be defined within a `<FORM>` tag and can be used to perform an action.

```
<INPUT TYPE="button" NAME="buttonName"
➥VALUE="textOnButton" [onClick="eventHandler"]>
```

When accessed from within a form, the form name is understood. To avoid confusion and create clearer code, it's preferred to use the form name with form elements. Used with an onClick event handler, a button becomes a custom item that can initiate events and activities beyond the basic submit and reset.

The following button invokes the `validateForm` function when the button is pressed.

```
<INPUT TYPE="button" NAME="validate" VALUE="Check
➥for Accuracy" onClick="validateForm(this.form)">
```

Related Items

Property of `form`.

See the `reset` and `submit` objects.

See the `name` and `value` properties.

See the `click` method.

See the `onClick` event handler.

ceil

(Method)

Returns the next integer larger than the argument.

```
Math.ceil(argument)
```

Usage

`ceil` returns the smallest integer greater than or equal to the integer or floating-point decimal passed to it as an argument. For example:

```
Math.ceil(1.01)
```

returns a 2.

Related Items

Method of `Math`.

See the `floor` method.

charAt

(Method)

Returns a character from a string.

```
stringName.charAt(index)
```

Usage

This method accepts an index as its argument and returns the character to that position in the string. The first character is at position 0 and the last at length −1.

```
var userName = "Bobba Louie"
document.write(userName.charAt(4))
```

returns an "a."

Related Items

Method of `string`.

See the `indexOf` and `lastIndexOf` methods.

checkbox

(Object)

A form element that the user sets to *on* or *off* by clicking it (see fig. QR.2).

```
formName.checkboxName
forms[index].elements[index]
```

☐ Please add me to the list.

Fig. QR.2   A form checkbox can only have two values, `true` or `false`. If the box is not checked, as shown here, its value is false. Otherwise, it's true.

Usage

Checkboxes are defined within a `<FORM>` tag.

```
<INPUT TYPE="checkbox" NAME="checkboxName"
➥VALUE="checkboxValue"
[CHECKED] [onClick="eventHandler"]> textToDisplay
```

The properties and methods of `checkboxes` are used in a variety of ways.

Use the `checked` value of `checkbox` to see if it is currently selected (`true`) or not (`false`). If the `CHECKED` option is used as part of the definition, `defaultChecked` also returns `true`.

Related Items

Property of `form`.

See the `radio` object.

checkbox

See the `checked`, `defaultChecked`, `name`, and `value` properties.

See the `click` method.

See the `onClick` event handler.

checked

(Property)

Returns a Boolean flag representing an individual checkbox or radio button status.

```
formName.checkboxName.checked
formName.radioButtonName[index].checked
forms[index].elements[index].checked
```

Usage

`checked` returns a Boolean value (`true` or `false`) indicating whether a checkbox or radio button is selected. The value is updated immediately when an item is checked. Used with the `for...in` statement, it can check the status of buttons:

```
function whichOneChecked() {
    var checkedValue = ""
    for (var i in document.formName.radioName) {
            if(document.formName.radioName[i]
.checked==true)

    checkedValue=document.formName.radioName[i].value
    }
}
```

Related Items

Property of `checkbox` and `radio`.

See the `defaultChecked` property.

clear

(Method)

Clears window contents, as a clear screen does.

```
document.clear()
```

Usage

`clear` erases the contents of a window, regardless of how the window was filled.

Related Items

Method of `document`.

See the `close`, `open`, `write`, and `writeln` methods.

clearTimeout

(Method)

Cancels a timeout.

```
[windowName.]clearTimeout(argument)
parent.[frameName.]clearTimeout(argument)
```

Usage

`clearTimeout` removes a timeout that was previously set using the `setTimeout` method. A timeout is set using a unique timeout ID that must be used to clear it:

```
clearTimeout(waitTime)
```

Related Items

Method of `frame` and `window`.

See the `setTimeout` method.

click

(Method)

Simulates a mouse click.

```
formName.elementName.click()
forms[index].elements[index].click()
```

Usage

The effect of a click depends on the type of form element that is referenced.

Table 4.1 The Click Method and Its Effect on Form Elements	
Form Element	**Action**
Button, Reset, and submit	Same as clicking button
Radio	Selects radio button
Checkbox	Marks checkbox and sets value to *on*

Related Items

Method of button, checkbox, radio, reset, and submit.

close

(Method)

For a document object, closes the current stream of output and forces its display.

For a window object, closes the current window.

```
document.close()
window.close()
[windowName.]close()
```

Usage

For documents, `close` stops the winsock browser's animation and displays "Document: Done" in the status bar.

For windows, as with all window commands, the `window` object is assumed. For example:

```
window.close()
close()
self.close()
```

all close the current window.

Related Items

Method of `document` and `window`.

See the `clear`, `open`, `write`, and `writeln` methods.

confirm

(Method)

Displays a JavaScript confirmation dialog box (see fig. QR.3).

```
window.confirm()
[windowName.]confirm()
```

Fig. QR.3 The JavaScript confirmation box allows a user to continue or to cancel out of an operation.

Usage

Similar to an `alert` with the addition of a Cancel button, `confirm` displays a message and a button to continue. `confirm` returns a `true` if the user selects OK and a `false` for Cancel. The following example loads a new window if the user presses OK:

confirm

```
if (confirm("Are you sure you want to enter.") {
   tourWindow = window.open("http:\\www.haunted.com
\","hauntedhouse")
}
```

Related Items

Method of `window`.

See the `alert` and `prompt` methods.

cookie

(Property)

String value of a small piece of information stored by Navigator in a client-side cookies.txt file.

```
document.cookie
```

Usage

The value stored in the `cookie` is found by using substring `charAt`, `IndexOf`, and `lastIndexOf`.

The cookie is a special property containing state/status information about the client that can be accessed by the server. Included in that `state` is a description of the range of URLs for which that state is valid.

Future HTTP requests from the client falling within a range of URLs described within the state object will include transmission of the current value of the state object from the client back to the server.

This simple form of data storage allows the server to provide personalized service to the client. Online merchants can store information about items currently in an electronic shopping basket, services can post registration information and automate functions such as typing a user ID.

User preferences can be saved on the client and retrieved by the server when the site is contacted. For limited-use information such as shopping services, you can also set a time limit on the life of the cookie information.

To post and view cookie settings within an HTML script, assign a value to the property.

```
document.cookie = "string"
```

CGI scripts are also used to set and retrieve cookie values. Generating the cookie requires sending an HTTP header in the format:

```
Set-Cookie: NAME=Value; [EXPIRES=date;]
➥[PATH=pathname;] [DOMAIN=domainname;] [SECURE]
```

When a request for cookie information is made, the list of cookie information is searched for all URLs that match the current URL. Any matches are returned in this format:

```
cookie: NAME1=string1; NAME2=string2; ...
```

Cookie was an arbitrarily assigned name. For more information about the cookie and its function, see Netscape's Cookie Specification at **http://home.netscape.com/newsref/std/cookie_spec.html**.

Related Items

Property of document.

See the hidden object.

COS

(Method)

Returns the cosine of the argument.

```
Math.cos(argument)
```

Usage

Angle size must be expressed in radians and the result is from −1 to 1.

Related Items

Method of Math.

See the acos, asin, atan, sin, and tan methods.

Date

(Object)

Provides a set of methods for working with dates and times.

```
Date.method(parameters)
```

Usage

The built-in `Date` object replaces a normal date type. Although it does not have any properties, the built-in `Date` object is equipped with a range of methods to set and change the values of its values.

Although date values are returned in standard form and syntax, the actual value is stored as the number of milliseconds since midnight on 1/1/70. The use of this convention prohibits the use of dates before 1/1/70.

To create a new `Date` object, use one of the following syntax conventions:

```
objectName = new Date() //Creates object with
➥current date and time
objectName = new Date("month day, year ➥[hours:
minutes:seconds]")
    //Creates date object with date and time values
➥in string variable or constant
objectName = new Date(year, month, day [, hours,
➥minutes, seconds])
    //Creates date object with integer values
```

If you omit the time component when you create a `Date` object, it defaults to midnight (00:00:00). Methods for getting and setting time and date information are divided into four classes: `set`, `get`, `to`, and `parse/UTC`.

Except for the day of the month, all numerical representations of date components begin numbering with 0. This should not present a problem except with months, which are represented by 0 (January) through 11 (December).

The standard date syntax is `"Thu, 11 Jan 1996 06:20:00 GMT"`. U.S. time zone abbreviations are also understood; but for universal use, specify the time zone offset. For example, `"Thu, 11 Jan 1996 06:20:00 GMT+0530"` is a place 5 hours and 30 minutes west of the Greenwich meridian.

Related Items

See the `getDate`, `getDay`, `getHours`, `getMinutes`, `getMonth`, `getSeconds`, `getTime`, `getTimezoneOffset`, `getYear`, `parse`, `setDate`, `setHours`, `setMinutes`, `setMonth`, `setSeconds`, `setTime`, `setYear`, `toGMTString`, `toLocaleString`, and `toUTC` methods.

defaultChecked

(Property)

A Boolean value (`true` or `false`) indicating whether a checkbox or radio button is checked by default.

```
formName.elementName.defaultChecked
forms[index].elements[index].defaultChecked
```

Usage

Setting a value to `defaultChecked` can override the checked attribute of a form element. The following section of code resets a group of radio buttons to their original state by finding and setting the default button:

```
for (var i in menuForm.choices) {
   if (menuForm.choices[i].defaultChecked) {
      menuForm.choices[i].defaultChecked = true
}
}
```

The button display is not affected with a change in the `defaultChecked` even if the status of other buttons are affected.

defaultChecked

Related Items

Property of `checkbox` and `radio`.

See the `form` object.

See the `checked` property.

defaultSelected

(Property)

Default state of an item in a form select element.

```
formName.elementName.defaultSelected
forms[index].elements[index].defaultSelected
```

Usage

`defaultSelected` returns a `true` or a `false`, depending on whether or not the `CHECKED` option was used with a `select` form element. Setting a value with this property can override the selected attribute of an `<OPTION>` tag. The syntax and behavior are identical to those of `defaultChecked`.

Related Items

Property of `options`.

See the `index`, `selected`, and `selectedIndex` properties.

defaultStatus

(Property)

The default message displayed in the status bar at the bottom of a Navigator window (see fig. QR.4).

```
[windowName.]defaultStatus
```

Fig. QR.4 The window status bar, which can hold predefined text other than a link URL.

Usage

Sets the message in the status bar when nothing else is displayed. This is preempted by a priority or transient message such as a `mouseOver` event with an `anchor`. For example:

```
window.defaultStatus = "Welcome to my home page"
```

displays the welcome message while the mouse is not over a link or Netscape is not performing an action that it needs to notify the user about.

Related Items

Property of `window`.

See the `status` property.

defaultValue

(Property)

The initial contents of text-type form elements.

```
formName.elementName.defaultValue
forms[index].elements[index].defaultValue
```

Usage

For any of the standard HTML text form fields—`hidden`, `password`, `text`, `textarea` (between the `<TEXTAREA>` tags), and `string`— defaultValue returns the initial contents, regardless of the current value. For password elements, this property is initially set to null for security reasons, regardless of any set `value`.

Related Items

Property of `hidden`, `password`, `text`, and `textarea`.

See the `value` property.

document

(Object)

An object created by Navigator when a page is loaded.

```
document.propertyOrMethod
document.objectName.propertyOrMethod
```

Usage

`document` is one of the base objects of JavaScript and contains information on the current document such as title, background color, and forms. These properties are defined within `<BODY>` tags. Through `write` and `writeln`, `document` also provides methods for displaying HTML text to the user.

You can reference the anchors, forms, and links of a document by using the appropriate arrays of the `document` object. These arrays contain an entry for each `anchor`, `form`, or `link` in a document.

Related Items

Property of `window`.

See the `frame` object; the `alinkColor`, `anchors`, `bgColor`, `cookie`, `fgColor`, `forms`, `lastModified`, `linkColor`, `links`, `location`, `referrer`, `title`, and `vlinkColor` properties.

See the `clear`, `close`, `open`, `write`, and `writeln` methods.

See the `onLoad` and `onUnload` event handlers.

E

(Property)

The base of natural logarithms.

```
Math.E
```

Usage

Also called *Euler's constant*, this value is approximately 2.71828.

Related Items

Property of `Math`.

See the LN2, LN10, LOG2E, LOG10E, PI, SQRT1_2, and SQRT2 properties.

elements

(Property)

An array of objects containing form elements in HTML source order.

```
formName.elements[index]
forms[index].elements[index]
```

Usage

The array index begins with 0 and ends with the number of `form` elements −1. For a complete discussion on `elements`, see the `elements` object.

Related Items

Property of `form`.

See the `elements` object.

elements array

(Object)

An array of `form` elements in source order.

```
formName.elements[index]
forms[index].elements[index]
```

Usage

All elements of a form are included in this array, which is accessible through the form name or the `forms` array. Form elements include buttons, checkboxes, radio buttons, text, and textarea objects. The elements can be referenced by their index.

For example, if a form contains two text fields, three radio buttons, and two push buttons, they are referenced in the `elements` array as `formName.elements[0]` through `formName.elements[6]`. Note that numbering begins with 0 and not 1.

To find the number of elements in a form, use the `length` property. The value of a member of the element array is the complete HTML text used to create it.

Elements can also be referenced by the element name. For example, a password element called newPassword is the second form element on an HTML page. Its value is accessed in three ways:

```
formName.elements[1].value
formName.elements["newPassword"].value
formName.newPassword.value
```

Values cannot be set or changed using the read-only `elements` array.

Related Items

Property of `form`.

See the `length` property.

encoding

(Property)

Returns a string reflecting the MIME encoding type.

```
formName.encoding
forms[index].encoding
```

Usage

MIME encoding types are set in the `enctype` attribute of an HTML `<FORM>` tag. The standards for MIME encoding in HTML are not established, but progress and draft documents are located at the University of California-Irvine Information and Computer Sciences Department, found on the Web at **http://www.ics.uci.edu/pub/ietf/html/**.

Related Items

Property of `form`.

See the `action`, `method`, and `target` properties.

escape*

(Method)

Returns the ASCII code of its argument.

```
escape(argument)
```

Usage

HTML ASCII codes are based on the ISO Latin −1 character set in the form %**xxx** where **xxx** is the decimal ASCII code. This method is not associated with any other object but is actually a native part of the JavaScript language. Alphanumeric characters (letters and numbers) will return as themselves, while symbols are returned as their ASCII code.

```
document.write(escape("Hi!"))
```

returns

```
Hi%21
```

Related Items

See the unescape method.

eval*

(Method)

Evaluates a string as a numeric expression.

```
eval(string)
```

Usage

This built-in function takes a string or numeric expression as its argument. If a string, eval tries to convert it to a numeric expression, then evaluates the expression and returns the value.

```
var x = 10
var y = 20
document.write(eval("x + y"))
```

This method can also be used to perform JavaScript commands included as part of a string.

```
var doThis = "if (x==10) { alert('Your maximum has
➥been reached') }
function checkMax () {
    x++;
    eval(doThis)
}
```

This can be useful when converting a date from a form (always a string) into a numerical expression or number.

exp

(Method)

Returns a natural logarithm.

```
Math.exp(argument)
```

Usage

exp returns the argument raised to the power of E (Euler's constant) to compute a natural logarithm.

Related Items

Method of Math.

See the log and pow methods.

See the E property.

fgColor

(Property)

The color of foreground text.

```
document.fgColor
```

Usage

Colors in JavaScript are represented as a hexadecimal RGB triplet or a string literal. This value cannot be changed after a document is processed, although it can be changed for individual sections of text with the fontcolor method.

fgColor takes two forms:

```
document.fgColor="aliceblue"
document.fgColor="F0F8FF"
```

which has the same effect as the TEXT attribute in the <BODY> tag:

```
<BODY TEXT="aliceblue">
```

Related Items

Property of document.

See the alinkColor, bgColor, linkColor, and vlinkColor properties.

See the fontcolor method.

fixed

(Method)

Formats the calling string into a fixed-pitch font.

```
stringName.fixed()
```

Usage

Using `fixed` is identical to encasing a string argument in HTML `<TT>` tags.

Related Items

Method of `string`.

floor

(Method)

Returns the next integer smaller than the argument.

```
Math.floor(argument)
```

Usage

Passing an integer or floating-point decimal to this method returns an integer less than or equal to its argument. For example:

```
Math.floor(2.99)
```

returns a 2.

Related Items

Method of `Math`.

See the `ceil` method.

focus

(Method)

Gives focus to a specific form element.

```
formName.elementName.focus()
forms[index].elements[index].focus()
```

Usage

Using the name of the form and the element, focus gives the element focus. From that point, a value can be entered by JavaScript commands or the user can complete the entry.

Related Items

Method of password, select, text, and textarea.

See the blur and select methods.

fontcolor

(Method)

Overrides the default foreground color for a string object.

```
stringName.fontcolor()
```

Usage

fontcolor formats the string object to a specific color expressed in the argument as a hexadecimal RGB triplet or a string literal. Using fontcolor is like using <FONT COLOR=COLOR>.

```
myDog = "Brown";
document.write(myDog.fontcolor("sienna"))
```

Related Items

Method of string.

fontsize

(Method)

Formats the string object to a specific font size.

stringName.fontsize(*argument*)

Usage

This method uses one of seven defined sizes using an integer through the <FONTSIZE=*SIZE*> tag. If a string is passed, then the size is changed relative to the value set in the <BASEFONT> tag.

The argument represents the size. If it is an integer, it is the size of the font and must be a number from 1 to 7. If it is a string, it changes the size of the font relative to the base font.

Related Items

Method of string.

See the big and small methods.

form (forms array)

(Object)

An object representing a form on a page.

document.*formName*
document.forms[*index*]

Usage

form is a property of the document object. Each form in a document is a separate and distinct object that can be referenced using the name of the form as the form object. The form object is also represented as an array created as forms are defined through HTML tags.

If the first form in a document is named orderForm, then it could be referenced as document.orderForm or document.forms[0]. If no name is given to the form, it can only be referenced by its index in the forms array. The number of individual forms on a page is available by using the `length` property.

```
document.forms.length
```

Individual elements of the form are referenced by their name or by using the `elements` array.

```
document.formName.elements[index]
```

The forms array is a read-only object. Attempts to set the value through statements such as:

```
document.forms[1]="OldGuestBook"
```

have no effect.

The value of an item in the forms array is presented in syntax similar to the syntax of HTML tags. For example, the value of the `form` object for a form with the name `userInfo` is `<OBJECT USERINFO>`.

Related Items

Property of `document`.

See the `hidden` object, the `action`, `elements`, `encoding`, `forms`, `method`, `name`, and `target` properties.

See the `submit` method.

See the `onSubmit` event handler.

forms

(Property)

An array of objects corresponding to named forms in HTML source order.

```
document.forms
```

Usage

`forms` are a property of the `document` object and contain an entry for each `form` object in a document. For a detailed discussion, see the `form` object.

Related Items

Property of `document`.

See the `form` object.

See the `length` property.

forward

(Method)

Loads the next document on the URL history list.

```
history.forward()
```

Usage

This method is the same as `history.go(1)`.

Related Items

Method of `history`.

See the `back` and `go` methods.

frame

(Object)

A window containing HTML subdocuments that are independently scrollable (see fig. QR.5).

```
[windowName.] [parent.] frameName
[windowName.] [parent.] frames[index]
```

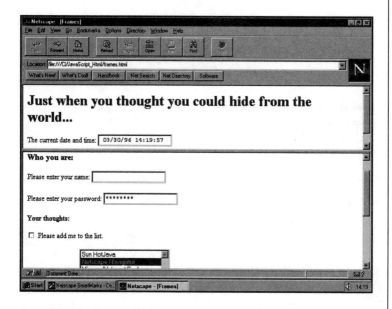

Fig. QR.5 A set of frames in a navigator window. Each frame contains its own HTML document.

Usage

Frames can point to different URLs and be targeted by other frames— all in the same window. Each `frame` is a `window` object defined using the `<FRAMESET>` tag to define the layout that makes up the page. The page is defined from a parent HTML document. All subdocuments are children of the parent.

If a `frame` contains definitions for `SRC` and `NAME` attributes, then the `frame` can be identified from a sibling by using the `parent` object as `parent.frameName` or `parent.frames[index]`.

Related Items

Property of `window`.

See the `document` and `window` objects.

the defaultStatus, frames, parent, self, status, top, and window properties.

See the setTimeout and clearTimeout methods.

frames

(Property)

An array corresponding to child frame windows created using the <FRAMESET> tag.

```
[windowName.][parent.]frameName
[windowName.][parent.]frames[index]
```

Usage

To obtain the number of child frames in a window, use the length property. For more information on the frames array, see the frame object.

Related Items

Property of window.

See the frame object.

See the length property.

getDate

(Method)

Returns the day of the month.

```
Date.getDate()
```

Usage

One of the few items in JavaScript that doesn't begin with a 0, this method returns a number between 1 and 31 representing the day of the month.

```
endOfTheWorld = new Date("January 11, 1996
➥06:18:00")
document.write(endOfTheWorld.getDate()) //Returns
➥11
```

Related Items

Method of `Date`.

See the `setDate` method.

getDay

(Method)

Returns the day of the week as an integer from 0 (Sunday) to 6 (Saturday).

```
Date.getDay()
dateName.getDay()
```

Usage

There is no corresponding `setDay` command because the day is automatically computed when the date value is assigned.

Related Items

Method of `Date`.

getHours

(Method)

Returns the hour of the day.

```
Date.getHours()
dateName.getHours()
```

Usage

The value is returned in 24-hour format, from 0 (midnight) to 23 (11 PM).

Related Items

Method of `Date`.

See the `setHours` method.

getMinutes

(Method)

Returns the minutes with an integer from 0 to 59.

```
Date.getMinutes()
dateName.getMinutes()
```

Usage

Like the other date functions, `getMinutes` is a straightforward matter of returning one element of the time.

```
endOfTheWorld = new Date("January 11, 1996
➥06:18:00")
document.write(endOfTheWorld.getMinutes()) //
➥Returns 18
```

Related Items

Method of `Date`.

See the `setMinutes` method.

getMonth

(Method)

Returns the month of the year.

```
Math.getMonth()
dateName.getMonth()
```

Usage

The month is returned as an integer between 0 (January) and 11 (December), not as a string. The value can be confusing since it doesn't follow conventional numbering for months of the year. When sending the value to the screen or prompting it from the user, be sure to make the conversion.

```
function toReality() { //converts month to 1-12
➥numbering system
    this += 1
}

function toConvention() { //converts month to 0-11
➥numbering system
    this -= 1
}
```

Related Items

Method of Date.

See the setMonth method.

getSeconds

(Method)

Returns the seconds.

```
Date.getSeconds()
dateName.getSeconds()
```

Usage

Seconds are returned as an integer from 0 to 59.

Related Items

Method of `Date`.

See the `setSeconds` method.

getTime

(Method)

Returns an integer representing the current value of the date object.

```
Date.getTime()
dateName.getTime()
```

Usage

The value is the number of milliseconds since midnight, Jan. 1, 1970. This value can be used to compare the length of time between two date values.

For functions involving computation of dates, it is useful to create a set of variables defining minutes, hours, and days in milliseconds:

```
var dayMillisec = 1000 * 60 * 60 * 24   //1,000
➼milliseconds x 60 sec x 60 min x 24 hrs
var hourMillisec = 1000 * 60 * 60   //1,000 milli-
➼seconds x 60 sec x 60 min
var minuteMillisec = 1000 * 60   //1,000 millisec-
➼onds x 60 sec
```

Related Items

Method of `Date`.

See the `setTime` method.

getTimezoneOffset

(Method)

Returns the difference in minutes between the client machine and Greenwich mean time (GMT).

```
Date.getTimezoneOffset()
dateName.getTimezoneOffset()
```

Usage

This value is a constant except for daylight savings time.

Related Items

Method of Date.

getYear

(Method)

Returns the year of the date object minus 1900.

```
Date.getYear()
dateName.getYear()
```

Usage

Although the year can be passed to a date object as a 4-digit number in a string, the value is returned from getYear as a 2-digit number. For example, 1996 is returned as 96.

Related Items

Method of Date.

See the setYear method.

go

(Method)

Loads a document specified in the history list.

```
history.go(argumentOrURL)
```

Usage

This method can reference documents in the history list by URL or relative to the current position on the list. If the URL is incomplete, then the closest match is used. The search is not case-sensitive.

Related Items

Method of `history`.

See the `back` and `forward` methods.

hash

(Property)

Returns a string with the portion of a URL beginning with a hash mark (#).

```
document.linkName.hash
document.links[index].hash
document.location.hash
```

Usage

Hashes denote an `anchor` name fragment. They can be used to set a `hash` property, although it is safest to set the entire URL as an `href` property. An error is returned if the `hash` isn't found in the current location.

Related Items

Property of `link` and `location`.

See the `anchor` object.

See the `host`, `hostname`, `href`, `pathname`, `port`, `protocol`, and `search` properties.

hidden

(Object)

A text object suppressed from appearing on an HTML form.

```
document.formName.hiddenName
document.forms[index].elements[index].propertyOrMethod
```

Usage

The hidden object can be used in addition to cookies to pass name/value pairs for client/server communication. The difference between the two is that cookies are persistent on the client between session, whereas the hidden object is specific to the form.

The initial contents of the hidden object can be changed within a function by assigning new contents to its value property.

```
<INPUT TYPE="hidden" NAME="failedTries" VALUE="0">
... statements ...
function setRetry() {
    document.userPasswordForm.failedTries.value++
}
```

Each time the setRetry function is called, the value of the hidden object named failedTries is incremented by 1. This is also an example of the loose typecasting in JavaScript. Even though the value is initially a string, when the script sees the mathematical operator, it attempts to convert the value to an integer.

Related Items

Property of form.

See the cookie, defaultValue, name, and value properties.

history

(Object)

A list of previously visited URLs, identical to the browser's Go menu.

```
document.history
```

history

Usage

This object is derived from the Go menu and contains the URL information for previously visited pages. Its methods are used to navigate to any point on the list.

To determine the number of items on the list, use the `length` property:

```
document.history.length
```

Navigation is possible with relative movements on the list using the `forward` and `back` methods, similar to using the menu bar navigation buttons.

```
document.history.forward()
document.history.back()
```

The `go` method allows jumps on the list beyond simple forward and back movement, similar to selecting an address directly from the Go menu.

```
document.history.go(-2) //loads the page two links
➥ago
```

When you specify a window, the navigation in other windows or frames is controllable. The following example loads a new page from the `history` list in the `content` frame. Note that the name of the frame replaces the `document` notation.

```
parent.content.history.back() //loads the previous
➥page in the frame
```

Related Items

Property of `document`.

See the `location` object.

See the `length` property.

See the `back`, `forward`, and `go` methods.

host

(Property)

Returns a string formed by combining the `hostname` and `port` properties of a URL:

```
location.host
linkName.host
links[index].host
```

Usage

Provides a method for viewing and changing URL host properties of location-type objects. If a port is not specified, the `host` property is the same as the `hostname` property.

```
location.host = "www.montana.com:80"
```

Related Items

Property of `link` and `location`.

See the `hash`, `hostname`, `href`, `pathname`, `port`, `protocol`, and `search` properties.

hostname

(Property)

Returns or changes a string with the domain name or IP address of a URL.

```
location.hostname
linkName.hostname
links[index].hostname
```

Usage

This property is similar to the `host` property except that it doesn't include the port information. When the port property is null, the `host` and `hostname` properties are identical.

Although `hostname` can be changed at any time, it is recommended to change the entire URL at once. If the `hostname` can't be found, an error is returned.

Related Items

Property of `link` and `location`.

See the `hash`, `host`, `href`, `pathname`, `port`, `protocol`, and `search` properties.

href

(Property)

Returns a string with the entire URL of the current document.

```
location.href
linkName.href
links[index].href
```

Usage

All other `location` and `link` properties are substrings of `href`, which can be changed at any time.

The URL of the current document is reflected to the screen using `document.write`.

```
document.write("You are here: " + window.location
➥.href)
```

Related Items

Property of `link` and `location`.

See the `hash`, `host`, `hostname`, `pathname`, `port`, `protocol`, and `search` properties.

index

(Property)

Returns the index of a select element option.

```
formName.selectName.options[index].index
forms[index].elements[index].options[index].index
```

Usage

The position of the option in the select object, with numbering beginning at 0.

Related Items

Property of `select` (`options`) array.

See the `defaultSelected`, `selected`, and `selectedIndex` properties.

indexOf

(Method)

Returns the location of a specific character or string.

```
stringName.indexOf(character/string, startingPoint)
```

Usage

The search starts from a specific location. The first character of the string is specified as zero and the last is the string's `length` −1. If the string is not found, the method returns a −1.

The `startingPoint` is zero by default.

```
if (navigator.appVersion.indexOf('Unix') != -1)
    return true
```

Related Items

Method of `string`.

See the `charAt` and `lastIndexof` methods.

isNaN*

(Method)

Checks to see if an argument is not a number.

`isNaN(argument)`

Usage

For UNIX platforms only, this stand-alone function returns `true` if the argument is not a number. On all platforms except Windows, the `parseFloat` and `parseInt` return `NaN` when the argument is not a number.

Related Items

See the `parseFloat` and `parseInt` methods.

italics

(Method)

Formats a string object into italics.

`stringName.italics()`

Usage

`italics` are the same as encasing a string in HTML `<I>` tags.

Related Items

Method of `string`.

See the `blink`, `bold`, and `strike` methods.

lastIndexOf

(Method)

Returns the index of a character or string in a `string` by searching from the end.

stringName`.lastIndexOf()`

Usage

Returns the index of a character or string in a `string` object by looking backwards from the end of the string or a user-specified index. It returns a −1 if the string is not found.

```
if (navigator.appVersion.lastIndexOf('Win') != -1)
    return true
```

Related Items

Method of `string`.

See the `charAt` and `indexOf` methods.

lastModified

(Property)

A read-only string containing the date that the current document was last changed.

`document.lastModified`

Usage

This property is based on the attributes of the source file. The string is formatted in the standard form used by JavaScript (see the `Date` object). A common usage is:

```
dateModified = "This page last modified on " +
➥document.lastModified
document.write(dateModified.small())
```

Related Items

Property of document.

length

(Property)

An integer reflecting a length- or size-related property of an object.

```
formName.length
forms.length
formName.elements.length
forms[index].length
[windowName.]frameName.length
frameRef.frames.length
history.length
radioName.length
selectName.length
selectName.options.length
stringName.length
windowName.length
anchors.length
links.length
```

Usage

The meaning of the value returned by length is determined by the array or object to which it's applied.

Table 4.2 Length property results

Object/Array	Property Measured
history	Length of the history list
string	Integer length of the string; zero for a null string
radio	Number of radio buttons
anchors, forms, frames, links, options	Number of elements in the array

Related Items

Property of anchors, elements, forms, frame, frames, history, links, options, radio, string, and window.

link

(Method)

Creates a hypertext link to another URL.

stringName.link(*argument*)

Usage

Creates a new hyperlink by defining the <HREF> attribute and the text representing the link to the user.

```
linkText = "Wossamatta University";
linkURL = "http://www.wossamatta.edu/";
document.write("Rocky's alma mater is " +
➥linkText.link(linkURL))
```

Related Items

Method of string.

See the anchor METHOD.

link (links array)

(Object)

Text or an image defined as a hypertext link to another URL.

```
document.linkName
document.links[index]
```

Usage

A link is a location object and, as such, has the same properties and methods as a location object.

If a name is defined for the object, it is also defined as an anchor and given an entry in the `anchors` array.

```
<A HREF='http://www.cnet.com/'>c|net's front door</
➥A>
<A HREF='http://www.cnet.com/' NAME='cnet'>c|net's
front door</A>
```

In the above example, the first line only creates an entry in the `links` array. With the addition of the `NAME` attribute, an additional entry is created in the `anchors` array.

The `link` object is read-only. To create a new hypertext link, use the `link` method (method of `string`).

Related Items

Property of `document`.

See the `anchor` object.

See the `hash`, `host`, `hostname`, `href`, `length`, `pathname`, `port`, `protocol`, `search`, and `target` properties.

See the `link` method.

See the `onClick` and `onMouseOver` event handlers.

linkColor

(Property)

The hyperlink color displayed in the document.

```
document.linkColor
```

Usage

Colors are expressed as a hexadecimal RGB triplet or as a string literal. The color corresponds to the `link` attribute in the HTML `<BODY>` tag and cannot be changed after the document is processed.

```
document.write("The current link color is " +
➥document.linkColor)
```

Related Items

Property of `document`.

See the `alinkColor`, `bgColor`, `fgColor`, and `vlinkColor` properties.

links

(Property)

An array representing `link` objects.

```
document.links[index]
```

Usage

Links are defined in HTML using `<A HREF=URL>` tags. These are reflected in the links property with the first `link` identified as `document.links[0]`. For a more detailed description, see the `link` object.

Related Items

See the `link` object.

See the `anchors` and `length` properties.

LN2

(Property)

A constant representing the natural logarithm of 2.

```
Math.LN2
```

Usage

This value is approximately 0.69315.

Related Items

Property of `Math`.

See the E, LN10, LOG2E, LOG10E, PI, SQRT1_2, and SQRT2 properties.

LN10

(Property)

A constant representing the natural logarithm of 10.

`Math.LN10`

Usage

This value is approximately 2.30259.

Related Items

Property of `Math`.

See the E, LN2, LOG2E, LOG10E, PI, SQRT1_2, and SQRT2 properties.

location

(Object)

Complete URL information for the current document.

```
[WindowName.][frameName.]location.propertyName
parent.[frameName.]location.propertyName
```

Usage

`location` is used to determine the URL for any active document, including those in other browser windows or frames. If the window object is omitted, the current window is assumed.

Each property of `location` contains a different portion of the URL. There are six parts of the URL reflected in the `location` object:

protocol://hostname:port/pathname search#hash

Protocols include the initial portion of the address (http, mailto, ftp, etc.) up to and including the colon. Several additional protocols are included for JavaScript.

The `javascript` protocol evaluates the expression after the colon and tries to load the string value of its result. If there is no result or it is undefined, the current page remains.

```
javascript:parent.content.history.go(-1)
```

The `about` protocol provides three methods to view information about the browser. By itself, it is the same as selecting Help, About. The other two methods, `cache` and `plugins`, reflect the current status of the cache and information about installed plug-in applications.

```
about:cache
about:plugins
```

Don't confuse this object, which is a property of `window`, with the `location` property of `document`. Generally, they reflect the same value but the property can't be changed, whereas the properties of the object can be changed.

Related Items

Property of `window`.

See the `history` object.

See the `hash`, `host`, `hostname`, `href`, `location`, `pathname`, `port`, `protocol`, `search`, and `target` properties.

location

(Property)

Returns a string with the URL of the current document.

```
document.location
```

Usage

This read-only property (`document.location`) is different from the location `object` properties (`window.location.propertyName`), which can be changed.

Related Items

Property of document.

See the location object.

log

(Method)

Returns the natural logarithm (base E) of a positive numeric expression greater than 0.

```
Math.log(expression)
```

Usage

An out-of-range number always returns −1.797693134862316e+308.

Related Items

Method of Math.

See the exp and pow methods.

LOG2E

(Property)

A constant representing the base-2 logarithm of E.

```
Math.LOG2E
```

Usage

The value is approximately 1.44270.

Related Items

Property of Math.

See the E, LN2, LN10, LOG10E, PI, SQRT1_2, and SQRT2 properties.

LOG10E

(Property)

A constant representing the base-10 logarithm of E.

```
Math.LOG10E
```

Usage

The value is approximately .43429.

Related Items

Property of `Math`.

See the E, LN2, LN10, LOG2E, SQRT1_2, and SQRT2 properties.

Math

(Object)

A built-in object providing constants and mathematical functions.

```
Math.property
Math.method(arguments)
```

Usage

The `Math` object is divided into two parts—properties containing constants and methods for implementing functions. For example, to access the value of pi in an equation, use:

```
Math.PI
```

Standard trigonometric, logarithmic, and exponential functions are also included. All arguments in trigonometric functions are limited to radians. Several comparison operations are provided, such as `max`, for determining the greater of two numbers.

Since the purpose of the `Math` object is to provide a vehicle for math operations, there are no provisions for a constructor to create a duplicate math object.

Math

For functions needing extensive use of JavaScripts math functions and constants, it is tedious to include Math as part of each equation. The with statement simplifies the syntax for this type of situation. Note the difference in the following two sections of code. Both perform the same operations.

```
function Hard() {
    circleArea = Math.PI*(radius^2);
    radians = (degrees/360)*Math.PI;
    result = Math.cos(radians);
}
function Easy() {
    with Math {
            circleArea = PI*(radius^2);
            radians = (degrees/360)*PI;
            result = cos(radians);
    }
}
```

Related Items

See the E, LN10, LN2, PI, SQRT1_2, and SQRT2 properties.

See the abs, acos, asin, atan, ceil, cos, exp, floor, log, max, min, pow, random, round, sin, sqrt, and tan methods.

max

(Method)

Returns the greater of its two arguments.

```
Math.max(argument1, argument2)
```

Usage

Can accept any combination of numeric literals or variables, and returns the value of the largest. For example:

```
firstNum = 1
secondNum = 100
Math.max(firstNum,secondNum)
```

returns 100.

Related Items

Method of `Math`.

See the `min` method.

method

(Property)

Reflects the method attribute of an HTML `<FORM>` tag.

```
formName.method
forms[index].method
```

Usage

The returned value is either `get` or `post`. It can be set to a new value at any time.

The first function returns the current value of the form object, whereas the second function sets the method to the contents of `newMethod`.

```
function getMethod(formObj) {
    return formObj.method
}

function setMethod(formObj,newMethod) {
    formObj.method = newMethod
}
```

Related Items

Property of `form`.

See the `action`, `encoding`, and `target` properties.

min

(Method)

Returns the lesser of its two arguments.

```
Math.min(argument1, argument2)
```

min

Usage

Can accept any combination of literals and variables as its argument, and returns the smaller number. For example:

```
firstNum = 1
secondNum = 100
Math.min(firstNum,secondNum)
```

returns 1.

Related Items

Method of `Math`.

See the `max` method.

name

(Property)

Returns a string with the `name` attribute of the object.

```
objectName.name
frameRef.name
frameRef.frames.name
radioName[index].name
selectName.options.name
windowRef.name
windowRef.frames.name
```

Usage

The attribute of this property depends on the object it is applied to. It can be changed at any time.

This property refers to the internal name for the `button`, `reset`, and `submit` objects, not the on-screen label.

For example, after opening a new window with:

```
indexOutline = window.open("http://
➥www.wossamatta.com/outline.html","MenuPage")
```

and issuing the command

```
document.write(indexOutline.name)
```

JavaScript returns `MenuPage`, which was specified as the name attribute.

For radio buttons, the name is the same for each button in the group, whereas individual buttons are identified by their position in the index.

Related Items

Property of `button`, `checkbox`, `frame`, `password`, `radio`, `reset`, `select`, `submit`, `text`, `textarea`, and `window`.

See the `value` property.

navigator

(Object)

Contains information on the client's current browser.

```
navigator
```

Usage

The `navigator` object returns version information about the browser, such as version number, name, and user-agent header. One common use is to determine the type of platform in use by the client so browser-specific features, such as newline characters and random numbers, are correctly used.

```
function UnixMachine() {
    if (navigator.appVersion.lastIndexOf('Unix') !=
➨-1)
          return true
    else
          return false
}
```

Related Items

See the `link` and `anchors` objects.

See the `appName`, `appCodeName`, `appVersion`, and `userAgent` properties.

onBlur

(Event Handler)

Occurs when a `select`, `text`, or `textarea` form element loses focus.

```
<INPUT TYPE="elementType" onBlur="function">
```

Usage

A blur event can check input as a user leaves the element. This is different from `onChange`, which only occurs if the contents of the field have changed.

```
<INPUT TYPE="textarea" VALUE="" NAME="feedback"
➡onBlur="checkSignature(this.value)">
```

Related Items

Event handler of `select`, `text`, `textarea`.

See the `focus` and `blur` methods.

See the `onChange` and `onFocus` event handlers.

onChange

(Event Handler)

Occurs when the value of a `select`, `text`, or `textarea` form element changes and loses focus.

```
<INPUT TYPE="elementType" onChange="function">
```

Usage

This event is especially useful for validating user form input.

```
<INPUT TYPE="text" VALUE="MT" NAME="state"
➡onChange="checkAvailability(this.value)">
```

Related Items

Event handler of `select`, `text`, `textarea`.

See the `onBlur` and `onFocus` event handlers.

onClick

(Event Handler)

Occurs when a clickable object is selected with the mouse.

```
<INPUT TYPE="elementType" onClick="function">
```

Usage

`onClick` offers a variety of functionality to buttons and other objects on a page. Buttons can be used to validate input before submitting or to compute the results of a form or equation. Clicking other objects, such as checkboxes and radio buttons, can trigger the capture of other information.

The following example sends the contents of the `overtime` form to the `howRich` function.

```
<FORM NAME="overtime">
Full days worked: <INPUT TYPE="text" VALUE="0"
➡NAME="days" SIZE=3>
Hours worked: <INPUT TYPE="text" VALUE="0"
➡NAME="hours" SIZE=30>
<INPUT TYPE="button" VALUE="Compute" NAME=
➡"computeWage" onClick="howRich(this.form)">
</FORM>
```

Related Items

Event handler of button, checkbox, radio, link, reset, and submit.

onFocus

(Event Handler)

Occurs when the user chooses a select, text, or textarea for input.

```
<INPUT TYPE="inputType" onFocus="function">
```

Usage

A form element receives focus when the user tabs to or clicks the input area with the mouse. Selecting within a field results in a select event.

One use of the onFocus function is for pop-up help when an item is selected for the first time.

Related Items

Event handler of select, text, and textarea.

See the onBlur and onChange event handlers.

onLoad

(Event Handler)

Occurs when a document finishes loading into a window or frameset.

```
<BODY onLoad="function">
<FRAMESET onLoad="function">
```

Usage

A load event is created when the browser finishes loading a window or all the frames within a <FRAMESET> tag.

Related Items

Event handler of `window`.

See the `onUnload` event handler.

onMouseOver

(Event Handler)

Occurs when a mouse is placed over a hyperlink.

```
<A HREF="URL" onMouseOver="function">linkText</A>
```

Usage

`onMouseOver` occurs when the mouse pointer is placed over a `link` object. To function with the `status` or `defaultStatus` properties, the event handler must return `true`.

```
<A HREF="http://home.netscape.com/"
onMouseOver="window.status='Netscape Home'; return
true">
Netscape</A>
```

Related Items

Event handler of `link`.

onSelect

(Event Handler)

`onSelect` occurs when text is highlighted within a form element.

```
<INPUT TYPE="textType" onSelect="function">
```

Usage

A select event is triggered by selecting some or all of the text in a `text` or `textarea` field.

Related Items

Event handler of `text` and `textarea`.

onSubmit

(Event Handler)

Occurs when a form is submitted by the user with the submit button.

```
<TAG onSubmit="function">
```

Usage

`onSubmit` is triggered when the user submits a form. Any return value other than `false`, including omitting the `return` statement, submits the form. To clarify the code, it is recommended to add `return` statements for both options.

```
<FORM onSubmit="feedbackSubmit()">
...form elements...
</FORM>

function feedbackSubmit () {
...statements...
if (!validData) {
    return true }
else {
    return false; }
}
```

Related Items

Event handler of `form`.

See the `submit` object.

See the `submit` method.

onUnload

(Event Handler)

Occurs when the user exits a document.

```
<BODY onUnload="function">
<FRAMESET onUnload="function">
```

Usage

When several unload events are included in a frame relationship, the order of operation proceeds from child to parent.

For example, an unload event is included with two documents and the parent <FRAMESET> tag that loaded them. When the child document changes, its unload event is triggered but the frameset unload is not affected. When the user selects an option that preempts the parent document for a new source, the top unload event is triggered.

Related Items

Event handler of window.

See the onLoad event handler.

open

(Method)

Creates a new document or window instance.

```
document.open([MIMEtype])
window.open("URL", "windowName" [,"windowFeatures"]
```

Usage

For a document, open opens a stream to collect the output of write or writeln methods. If the MIME type is a version of text or image such as text/html or image/gif, the document is opened for lay-out. Otherwise, the stream is routed to a plug-in. If a document already exists in the target window, then the open method clears it. The stream is ended by using the document.close() method.

open

For a window, open opens a new browser window in a similar fashion to choosing File, New Web Browser from the browser menu. Using the URL argument, it loads a document into the new window; otherwise, the new window is blank. When used as part of an event handler, the form must include the window object; otherwise, the document is assumed.

Window features are defined by a comma-separated list of options with =1 or =yes to enable and =0 or =no to disable. Window features include toolbar, location, directories, status, menubar, scrollbars, resizable, copyhistory, width, and height.

Related Items

Method of document and window.

See the clear, close, write, and writeln methods.

options

(Property)

This array of options is a property of a select form element. The array is created by using <OPTION> tags within a set of <SELECT> tags.

```
formName.selectName.options[index]
forms[index].elements[index].options[index]
```

Usage

The first option's index is zero, the second is 1, and so on. For more detailed information, see the select object.

Related Items

See select OBJECT.

parent

(Property)

Refers to the calling document in the current frame created by a <FRAMESET> tag.

```
parent
parent.frameName
parent.frames[index]
parent.property
```

Usage

Using `parent` allows access to other frames created by the same `<FRAMESET>` tag. For example, two frames invoked are called *index* and *contents*. The index frame can write to the contents frame using the syntax:

```
parent.contents.document.write("Kilroy was here.")
```

Related Items

Property of `frame` and `window`.

parse

(Method)

Takes a date string, such as `Jan 11, 1996`, and returns the number of milliseconds since midnight, Jan. 1, 1970.

Usage

This function can be used to set date values based on string values. When passed a string with a time, it returns the time value.

Because `parse` is a static function of `Date`, it is always used as `Date.parse()` rather than as a method of a created `Date` object.

```
Date.parse("Jan 11, 1996");
Today = new Date();
Date.parse(Today.toLocaleString())
Related Items
```

Method of `Date`.

See the `UTC` method.

82

parseFloat*

parseFloat*

(Method)

```
parseFloat(string)
```

Usage

parseFloat parses a string argument and returns a floating-point number if the first character is a plus sign, minus sign, decimal point, exponent, or a numeral.

If parseFloat encounters a character other than one of the valid choices after that point, it returns the value up to that location and ignores all succeeding characters. If the first character is not a valid character, parseFloat returns one of two values based on the platform:

```
Windows    0
Non-Windows     NaN
```

Related Items

See methods isNaN and parseInt.

parseInt*

(Method)

Parses a string argument and returns an integer based on a specified radix or base.

```
parseInt(string [,radix])
```

Usage

A radix of 10 converts the value to a decimal, whereas 8 converts to octal and 16 to hexadecimal. Values greater than 10 for bases above 10 are represented with letters A through F in place of numbers. Using a radix of 2 is used for binary number conversions.

Floating-point values are converted to integers. The rules for evaluating the string are identical to those for parseFloat.

If the radix is omitted or a radix which contradicts the initial characters, JavaScript assumes the radix based on the first characters of the string.

Table 4.3 Default radix based on the initial string characters.

Characters	Radix
0	8 (octal)
0x	16 (hexadecimal)
Any other	10 (decimal)

Related Items

See the isNaN and parseFloat methods.

password

(Object)

A password element in an HTML form (see fig. QR.6).

```
document.formName.passwordName
document.forms[index].element[index]
```

Please enter your password: `********`

Fig. QR.6 A password element is masked with asterisks for security.

Usage

A password is a text field that for security is masked with asterisks when entered by the user.

Any default values included as part of the HTML definition are cleared when the page is loaded. This prevents inadvertent or intentional security breaches. Even though the defaultValue property is valid for password, it always returns a null value.

The value of a password object can be evaluated programmatically within a script but it is recommended not to use a literal for obvious security reasons.

Related Items

Property of form.

See the text object.

See the defaultValue, name, and value properties.

See the focus, blur, and select methods.

pathname

(Property)

Returns the path portion from an URL.

```
location.pathname
link.pathname
links[index].pathname
```

Usage

Although the pathname can be changed at any time, it is always safer to change the entire URL at once using the href property.

Related Items

Property of link and location.

See the hash, host, hostname, href, port, protocol, and search properties.

PI

(Property)

Returns the value of pi.

```
Math.PI
```

Usage

The value of Math.PI is approximately 3.14159. This is the ratio of the circumference of a circle to its diameter.

```
circumference = 2 * Math.Π * radius
area = Math.Π * Math.pow(radius,2)
```

Related Items

Property of Math.

See the E, LN2, LN10, LOG2E, LOG10E, SQRT1_2, and SQRT2 properties.

port

(Property)

Returns the port number of an URL address.

```
location.port
link.port
links[index].port
```

Usage

The port value is a substring of the host property in href.

Related Items

Property of link and location.

See the hash, host, hostname, href, pathname, protocol, and search properties.

pow

(Method)

Returns a base raised to an exponent.

```
Math.pow(argument)
```

Usage

Many languages use the caret operator (^) to calculate an exponent. JavaScript includes its own method to do this. The caret is used in JavaScript to calculate a bitwise XOR operation.

Related Items

Method of Math.

See the exp and log methods.

prompt

(Method)

Displays a prompt dialog box that accepts user input (see fig. QR.7).

```
[windowName.]prompt(message [inputDefault])
```

Fig. QR.7 The prompt dialog box is used to get user input outside of a form.

Usage

If an initial value is not specified for inputDefault, the dialog box displays the <UNDEFINED> value. Generating the prompt in fig 4.7 required one line of code:

```
var userid = prompt("Please enter your ID","")
```

Related Items

Method of window.

See the alert and confirm methods.

protocol

(Property)

Returns the file access method.

```
location.protocol
link.protocol
links[index].protocol
```

Usage

The string returned by this property is the initial portion of a URL, up to and including the colon. This is the part of the URL that indicates the access method (`http`, `ftp`, `mailto`, etc.).

about	Information about the client browser.
ftp	A file transfer protocol address for downloading files.
http	Hypertext transfer address which is the basis of the World Wide Web.
mailto	An email address.
news	A usenet news site.
file	Refers to a file on the local machine.
javascript	Precedes a set of JavaScript commands.

Related Items

Property of `link` and `location`.

See the `hash`, `host`, `hostname`, `href`, `pathname`, `port`, and `search` properties.

radio

(Object)

A set of radio buttons.

```
formName.radioName[index]
forms[index].elements[index]
```

Usage

radio objects are created within HTML <FORM> tags and represent radio buttons. A set of radio buttons enables the user to select one item from a group of options.

When referencing the object using the radio button name, the index is comprised of the buttons with the same name property. When referring to a radio button using the elements array, each button is a separate item in the index.

Related Items

Property of form.

See the checkbox and select objects.

See the checked, defaultChecked, index, length, name, and value properties.

See the click method.

See the onClick event handler.

random

(Method)

Returns a random number between 0 and 1 (UNIX only).

```
Math.random()
```

Usage

The random method is only enabled on UNIX platforms—Windows and Macintosh users need to use an alternative form of generating a random number. An example of this type of usage is included in the Task Reference at the end of this book.

Related Items

Method of Math.

referrer

(Property)

URL of the document which led to the current document.

```
document.referrer
```

Usage

Returns a read-only string containing the complete URL of the document that called the current document. It can be used with a CGI script to keep track of how users are linked to a page.

```
document.write("Click <A HREF=\''"+document
➥.referrer+"\'>here</A> to go back from whence you
➥came.""> 
```

Related Items

Property of document.

reset

(Object)

Button to return a form to its default values.

```
formName.resetButtonName
forms[index].elements[index]
```

Usage

This button correlates with an HTML reset button, which resets all form objects to their default values.

A reset object must be created within a <FORM> tag and cannot be controlled through the onClick event handler. When the button is clicked, the form is reset. However, the event handler can invoke other actions with the reset.

Related Items

Property of `form`.

See the `button` and `submit` objects.

See the `name` and `value` properties.

See the `click` method.

See the `onClick` event handler.

round

(Method)

Rounds a number to the nearest integer.

```
Math.round(argument)
```

Usage

Returns the value of a floating-point argument rounded to the next highest integer if the decimal portion is greater than or equal to .5, or the next lowest integer if less than .5.

```
Math.round(2.1)   //Returns 2
Math.round(2.9)   //Returns 3
```

Related Items

Method of `Math`.

search

(Property)

Returns any query information attached to a URL.

```
location.search
linkName.search
links[index].search
```

Usage

Returns a string containing any query information appended to a URL. Query data is preceded by a question mark and is the last item included in the document URL. Information in the string is formatted this way:

```
?elementName=element+value
```

Like all substrings of the href property, search can be changed at any time.

Related Items

Property of link and location.

See the hash, host, hostname, href, pathname, port, and protocol properties.

select

(Method)

Selects the input area of a specified form element.

```
formName.elementName.select()
forms[index].elements[index].select()
```

Usage

Used with the focus method, JavaScript can highlight a field and position the cursor for user input.

Related Items

Method of password, text, and textarea.

See the blur and focus methods.

select (options array)

(Object)

A selection list or scrolling list on an HTML form (see fig. QR.8).

```
formName.selectName
forms[index].elements[index]
formName.selectName[index].options[index]
forms[index].elements[index].options[index]
```

Fig. QR.8 A drop-down selection list (left) from an HTML form allows one choice, whereas a scrolling list (right) allows multiple choices.

Usage

A selection list enables the user to choose one item from a list. A scrolling list enables the choice of one or more items from a list, enabled using the MULTIPLE attribute in the input tag.

When used without the options array, the select object refers to the entire list, using options such as length and name. The value and selectedIndex indicate the currently selected option in a selection list or the first selected item of a scrolling list.

Related Items

Property of form.

See the radio object.

See the length, name, options, and selectedIndex properties.

See the blur and focus methods.

See the onBlur, onChange, and onFocus event handlers.

For the options property of select, see the defaultSelected, index, selected, text, and value properties.

selected

(Property)

Returns a Boolean value (`true` or `false`) indicating the current state of an option in a `select` object.

```
formName.elementName.[options[index].]selected
forms[index].elements[index].[options[index].]selected
```

Usage

The selected property can be changed at any time and the display will immediately update to reflect the new value. The selected property is useful for `select` elements that are created using the `multiple` attribute.

Using the `select` property, you can view or change the value of any element in an `options` array without changing the value of any other element in the array.

Related Items

Property of `options`.

See the `defaultSelected`, `index`, and `selectedIndex` properties.

selectedIndex

(Property)

Returns an integer specifying the index of a selected item.

```
formName.elementName.[options[index].]selected
forms[index].elements[index].[options[index].]selected
```

Usage

The `selectedIndex` property is useful for `select` elements that are created without using the `MULTIPLE` attribute in the `<SELECT>` tag. If `selectedIndex` is evaluated when the `MULTIPLE` attribute is set, the property returns the index of the first option only. Setting the property clears any other options that are selected in the element.

Related Items

Property of `select`, `options`.

See the `defaultSelected`, `index`, and `selected` properties.

self

(Property)

Refers to the current window or form.

```
self
```

Usage

The `self` property is useful for removing ambiguity when dealing with `window` and `form` properties of the same name.

Related Items

Property of `frame` and `window`.

See the `window` property.

setDate

(Method)

Sets the day of the month.

```
Date.setDate(argument)
dateName.setDate(argument)
```

Usage

`setDate` uses an integer from 1 to 31 to set the day of the month for a Date object.

```
endOfTheWorld = new Date("January 11, 1996
➥06:18:00")
endOfTheWorld.setDate(26)
document.write(endOfTheWorld.getDate()) //Returns
➥26
```

Related Items

Method of `Date`.

See the `getDate` method.

setHours

(Method)

Sets the hour for the current time.

```
Date.setHours(argument)
dateName.setHours(argument)
```

Usage

`setHours` uses an integer from 0 (midnight) to 23 (11 p.m.) to set the hour of the day using military time.

Related Items

Method of `Date`.

See the `getHours` method.

setMinutes

(Method)

Sets the minutes for the current time.

```
Date.setMinutes(argument)
dateName.setMinutes(argument)
```

Usage

Uses an integer from 0 to 59 to set the minutes of a date object.

Related Items

Method of `Date`.

See the `getMinutes` method.

setMonth

(Method)

Sets the month value of a date object.

```
Date.setMonth(argument)
dateName.setMonth(argument)
```

Usage

Uses an integer from 0 (January) to 11 (December). This is the one item of the `Date` object that doesn't follow normal numbering conventions. Be sure to make the adjustment when transferring values from the JavaScript month to a form understandable by the user.

Related Items

Method of `Date`.

See the `getMonth` method.

setSeconds

(Method)

Sets the seconds.

```
Date.setSeconds(argument)
dateName.setSeconds(argument)
```

Usage

Uses an integer from 0 to 59 to set the seconds of a date object. Although the `Date` object uses milliseconds to track time, seconds are the greatest level of detail allowed when entering a specific time.

Related Items

Method of `Date`.

See the `getSeconds` method.

setTime

(Method)

Sets the value of a date object.

```
dateName.setTime(argument)
```

Usage

This is the base form of a `Date` object. It returns the number of milliseconds since midnight on Jan. 1, 1970. Although it is not necessary to know this number, it can be used as a simple method of copying the value of one date object to another.

```
endOfTheWorld = new Date(userGuess)
checkDate = new Date()
checkDate.setTime(endOfTheWorld.getTime())
```

Related Items

Method of `Date`.

See the `getTime` method.

setTimeout

(Method)

Evaluates an expression after a specified amount of time, expressed in milliseconds.

setTimeout

```
[window.]setTimeout(timerID)
[windowName.]setTimeout(timerID)
```

Usage

Timeouts are not repeated indefinitely. For example, setting a timeout
to 3 seconds evaluates the expression once after 3 seconds—not every
3 seconds.

To call setTimeout recursively, reset the timeout as part of the function invoked by the method. Calling the function startclock in the
following example sets a loop in motion that clears the timeout, displays the current time, and sets the timeout to redisplay the time in 1
second.

```
<SCRIPT>
var timerID = null;
var timerRunning = false;

function stopclock () {
  if(timerRunning) clearTimeout(timerID);
  timerRunning=false;
}
function startclock () {
  stopclock();
  showtime();
}
function showtime () {
  var now = new Date();
  document.clock.display.value = now.
➡toLocaleString();
  timerID = setTimeout("startclock()",1000);
  timerRunning = true;
}
</SCRIPT>

<BODY onLoad="startclock()">
<FORM NAME="clock">
<INPUT ITEM=text NAME="display" VALUE="Standby for
➡the time">
</FORM>
</BODY>
```

Related Items

Method of `window`.

See the `clearTimeout` method.

setYear

(Method)

Sets the year in the current date.

```
Date.setYear(argument)
dateName.setYear(argument)
```

Usage

`setYear` needs a 2-digit integer representing the year minus 1900.

Related Items

Method of `Date`.

See the `getYear` method.

sin

(Method)

Returns the sine of an argument.

```
Math.sin(argument)
```

Usage

The argument is the size of an angle expressed in radians and the returned value is from −1 to 1.

Related Items

Method of `Math`.

See the `acos`, `asin`, `atan`, `cos`, and `tan` methods.

small

(Method)

```
stringName.small()
```

Usage

small formats a string object into a small font using the HTML
<SMALL> tags.

Related Items

Method of string.

See the big and fontsize methods.

sqrt

(Method)

Returns the square root of a positive numeric expression.

```
Math.sqrt(argument)
```

Usage

If the argument's value is outside the range, the returned value is 0.

SQRT1_2

(Property)

The square root of 1/2.

```
Math.SQRT1_2
```

Usage

The square root of 1/2 is also expressed as the inverse of the square
root of 2 (approximately 0.707).

Related Items

Property of Math.

See the E, LN2, LN10, LOG2E, LOG10E, PI, and SQRT2 properties.

SQRT2

(Property)

The square root of 2.

```
Math.SQRT2
```

Usage

The value of this constant is approximately 1.414.

Related Items

Property of Math.

See the E, LN2, LN10, LOG2E, LOG10E, PI, and SQRT1_2 properties.

status

(Property)

Specifies a priority or transient message to display in the status bar.

```
window.status
[windowName].status
```

Usage

The status bar is located at the bottom of the window. A user status message is usually triggered by a mouseOver event from an anchor. To display a message in the status bar when the mouse pointer is placed over a link, the usage is:

```
<A anchorDefinition onMouseOver="window.status=
➥'Your message.'; return true">link</A>
```

Note the use of nested quotes and use of `return true`, needed for operation.

Once invoked, the message remains until the mouse is placed over another link.

Related Items

Property of `window`.

See the `defaultStatus` property.

strike

(Method)

Formats a string object as strikeout text.

`stringName.strike()`

Usage

Using `strike` is identical to using HTML `<STRIKE>` tags.

Related Items

Method of `string`.

See the `blink`, `bold`, and `italics` methods.

string

(Object)

A series of characters defined by double or single quotation marks.

`stringName`

Usage

For example:

```
myDog = "Brittany Spaniel"
```

returns a string object called `myDog` with the `Brittany Spaniel` value. Quotation marks are not a part of the string's value—they are only used to delimit the string.

The object's value is manipulated using methods that return a variation on the string—for example `myDog.toUpperCase()` returns BRIT-TANY SPANIEL. A string object also includes methods that return HTML versions of the string, such as `bold` and `italics`.

Related Items

See the `text` and `textarea` objects.

See the `length` property.

See the `anchor`, `big`, `blink`, `bold`, `charAt`, `fixed`, `fontcolor`, `fontsize`, `indexOf`, `italics`, `lastIndexOf`, `link`, `small`, `strike`, `sub`, `substring`, `sup`, `toLowerCase`, and `toUpperCase` methods.

sub

(Method)

Formats a string object into subscript text.

```
stringName.sub()
```

Usage

Using `sub` is identical to using HTML `<SUB>` tags.

Related Items

Method of `string`.

See the `sup` method.

submit

(Object)

A submit button on an HTML page.

formName.buttonName
forms[*index*].elements[*index*]

Usage

Clicking on the button causes the form to be submitted to the program specified by the action property. The button is created within an HTML <FORM> tag, and always loads a new page, which may be the same as the current page if an action isn't specified.

Related Items

Property of form.

See the button and reset objects.

See the name and value properties.

See the click method.

See the onClick event handler.

submit

(Method)

Performs the same action as clicking a submit button.

formName.submit()
forms[*index*].submit()

Usage

The information from the form is submitted depending on the attribute of the METHOD attribute—get or post.

Related Items

Method of `form`.

See the `submit` object.

See the `onSubmit` event handler.

substring

(Method)

Returns a subset of a string object based on two indexes.

`stringName.substring(index1, index2)`

Usage

If the indexes are equal, an empty string is returned. Regardless of order, the substring is built from the smallest index to the largest.

Related Items

Method of `string`.

sup

(Method)

Formats a string object into superscript text.

`stringName.sup()`

Usage

Using `sup` is identical to using HTML `<SUP>` tags.

Related Items

Method of `string`.

See the `sub` method.

tan

(Method)

Returns the tangent of an argument.

```
Math.tan(argument)
```

Usage

The argument is the size of an angle expressed in radians.

Related Items

Method of Math.

See the acos, asin, atan, cos, sin methods.

target

(Property)

A string specifying the name of a window for posting responses to after a form is submitted.

```
formName.target
forms[index].target
location.target
link.target
links[index].target
```

Usage

Normally used to view the destination for a form submission, target can also be used to view or change a link's destination. For a link, target returns a string specifying the name of the window that displays the content of a selected hypertext link.

```
homePage.target = "http://www.wossamatta.edu/"
```

You must use a literal to set the target property. JavaScript expressions and variables are invalid entries.

Related Items

Property of `form`, `link`, and `location`.

See the `action`, `encoding`, and `method` properties.

text

(Object)

A one-line input field on an HTML form (see fig. QR.9).

```
formName.textName
forms[index].elements[index]
```

Please enter your name: |

Fig. QR.9 Text input boxes are objects within the form.

Usage

`text` objects accept characters or numbers. A `text` object can be updated by assigning new contents to its value.

Related Items

Property of `form`.

See the `password`, `string`, and `textarea` objects.

See the `defaultValue`, `name`, and `value` properties.

See the `focus`, `blur`, and `select` methods.

See the `onBlur`, `onChange`, `onFocus`, and `onSelect` event handlers.

text

(Property)

Returns the value of text following the `<OPTION>` tag in a `select` object.

```
formName.selectName.options[index].text
forms[index].elements[index].options[index].text
```

Usage

`text` can also be used to change the value of the option, with an important limitation: although the value is changed, its appearance on-screen is not.

Related Items

Property of `options`.

textarea

(Object)

`textarea` is similar to a `text` object, with the addition of multiple lines (see fig. QR.10).

```
formName.textAreaName
forms[index].elements[index]
```

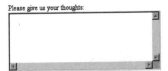

Fig. QR.10   The `textarea` object can accept multiple lines of text from the user.

Usage

A `textarea` object can also be updated by assigning new contents to its value. The screen is updated immediately after the new value is assigned.

```
<FORM>
<ITEM INPUT=textarea NAME="sponsorMessage"
➥VALUE="And now a brief message from our spon-
sor.">
</FORM>
```

```
...
<SCRIPT>
sponsorMessage.value = "Now is the time \r\n for
everybody to get up \r\n and run away."
</SCRIPT>
```

Note the use of the newline character \n. The implementation of a new line depends on the platform. For Windows, it's the combination \r\n; for Macintosh and UNIX, it's \n.

When defining a textarea in a form, you can load a default value by including text between the <TEXTAREA> tags. The following example loads three lines of text and a blank line into a textarea element.

```
<BR><TEXTAREA NAME="user_comments" ROWS=4 COLS=40>
Enter your comments here.

Or just press the submit button to let us
know you liked what you saw.
</TEXTAREA>
```

Related Items

Property of form.

See the password, string, and text objects.

See the defaultValue, name, and value properties.

See the focus, blur, and select methods.

See the onBlur, onChange, onFocus, and onSelect event handlers.

title

(Property)

Returns the read-only value set within HTML <TITLE> tags.

```
document.title
```

Usage

If a document doesn't include a title, the value is `null`.

Related Items

Property of `document`.

---

toGMTString

(Method)

Converts a date object to a string using the Internet GMT conventions.

```
Date.toGMTString()
dateName.toGMTString()
```

Usage

This string conversion returns a string containing the time in a GMT format, which can vary depending on the platform.

For example, if `today` is a date object:

```
today.toGMTString()
```

then the string "Thu, 11 Jan 1996 06:05:15" is returned. Actual formatting may vary from platform to platform. The time and date are based on the client machine.

Related Items

Method of `Date`.

See `toLocaleString` method.

---

toLocaleString

(Method)

Converts a date object to a string using the local conventions.

```
Date.toLocaleString()
dateName.toLocaleString()
```

Usage

The date string returned by this method depends on the preferences defined on the client machine, such as *mm/dd/yy hh:mm:ss*.

Related Items

Method of Date.

See the toGMTString method.

toLowerCase

(Method)

Converts all characters in a string to lowercase.

```
stringName.toLowerCase()
```

Usage

The results of the toLowerCase method are displayed entirely in lowercase characters although the actual contents of the string are not changed.

Related Items

Method of string.

See the toUpperCase method.

top

(Property)

The top-most browser window.

```
top
top.frameName
top.frames[index]
```

Usage

Also called an *ancestor* or *Web browser window*, the top property refers to the highest precedence window that contains `frames` or nested `framesets`.

Related Items

Property of `window`.

toUpperCase

(Method)

Converts all characters in a string to uppercase.

`stringName.toUpperCase()`

Usage

Although it affects the immediate display of the string, `toUpperCase` does not affect the value of its object.

Related Items

Method of `string`.

See the `toLowerCase` method.

unescape*

(Method)

Returns a character based on its ASCII value.

`unescape(string)`

Usage

The value returned is expressed as a string in the format %**xxx** where xxx is a decimal number between zero and 255, or 0x0 to 0xFF in hex.

Related Items

See the escape METHOD.

userAgent

(Property)

Header sent as part of HTTP protocol from client to server to identify the type of client.

```
navigator.userAgent
```

Usage

The syntax of the returned value is the same as for appVersion, with the addition of the browser application code name.

```
codename/releaseNumber (platform; country)
```

Related Items

Property of navigator.

See the appName, appVersion, and appCodeName properties.

UTC

(Method)

Returns the number of milliseconds for a universal coordinated time (UTC) date since midnight, January 1, 1970.

```
Date.UTC(year, month, day [, hrs] [, min] [, sec])
```

Usage

UTC is always calculated from the same date, and therefore, always used as Date.UTC(), not with a created date object. When including the value for the month, don't forget that JavaScript numbers the months from 0 to 11.

Related Items

Method of `Date`.

See the `parse` method.

value

(Property)

Returns the value of an object.

```
formName.buttonName.value
formName.resetName.value
formName.submit.value
formName.checkboxName.value
formName.radioName.value
formName.hiddenName.value
formName.textName.value
formName.textareaName.value
formName.selectName.value
formName.passwordName.value
forms[index].elements[index].value
```

Usage

The value of an object depends on the type of object it is applied to.

Table 4.4   Values of Various Form Objects

Object	Value Attribute
button, reset, submit	Value attribute that appears on-screen, not the button name
checkbox	*On* if item is selected, *off* if not
radio	String reflection of value
hidden, text, textarea	Contents of the field

`select`	Reflection of option value
`password`	Returns a valid default value, but an encrypted version if modified by the user

Changing the value of a `text` or `textarea` object results in an immediate update to the screen. All other `form` objects are not graphically updated when changed.

Related Items

Property of `button`, `checkbox`, `hidden`, `options`, `password`, `radio`, `reset`, `submit`, `text`, and `textarea`.

For `password`, `text`, and `textarea`, see the `defaultValue` property.

For `button`, `reset`, and `submit`, see the `name` property.

For `options`, see the `defaultSelected`, `selected`, `selectedIndex`, and `text` properties.

For `checkbox` and `radio`, see the `checked` and `defaultChecked` properties.

vlinkColor

(Property)

Returns or sets the color of visited links.

```
document.vlinkColor
```

Usage

Like all colors, `vlinkColor` uses hexadecimal RGB triplets or a string literal. The property cannot be set after the document has been formatted. To override the browser defaults, color settings are used with the `onLoad` event handler in the `<BODY>` tag:

vlinkColor

```
<BODY onLoad="document.vlinkColor='aliceblue'">
```

Related Items

Property of `document`.

See the `alinkColor`, `bgColor`, `fgColor`, and `linkColor` properties.

window

(Object)

The highest precedence object accessible by JavaScript relating to an open Navigator window.

```
window
self
top
parent
windowName
propertyName
methodName(parameters)
```

Usage

`window` is created by Navigator when a page is loaded containing properties that apply to the whole window. It is the top-level object for each `document`, `location`, and `history` object. Because its existence is assumed, you do not have to reference the name of the window when referring to its objects, properties, or methods.

For example, the following two lines have the same result (printing a message to the status line):

```
status="Go away from here."
window.status="Go away from here."
```

There are numerous ways of referencing a window, depending on its relation to the current location as outlined in Table 4.5.

Table 4.5 Window Aliases	
Window Name	**Reference**
window, self	The window containing the current document. When these aliases are omitted, the current document is still assumed. The exception is in scripting event handlers, where methods such as `open` and `close` must be used with specific windows or frames.
top	Refers to the top most window. Useful for parent-child-child relationships created with multiple `<FRAMESET>` tags.
parent	The window containing the `<FRAMESET>` tag that created the current window.
windowName	Used to reference the window in HTML tags. When using properties and methods of a window, use the name of the window variable.

A new window is created using the `open` method:

```
aNewWindow = window.open("URL","Window_Name"
➥[,"windowFeatures"])
```

The variable name is used to refer to the window's properties and methods. The window name is used in the target argument of a `form` or `anchor` tag. The list of features (Table 4.6) controls the appearance and functionality of the browser (see fig. QR.11).

If no features are listed, all are included by default. If any feature is explicitly defined, any not included in the feature list are excluded by default.

window

Table 4.6 Window Feature Attributes

Option	Use
toolbar	Includes standard toolbar, including forward, back, home, and print buttons.
location	Creates a location object.
directories	In Netscape, includes the list of buttons for standard links, such as What's New, What's Cool, and Handbook.
status	Creates a status bar at the bottom of the screen.
menubar	Includes the menubar at the top of the screen, including items such as File, Edit, and View.
scrollbars	Adds scrollbars if the document extends beyond the size of the screen.
resizable	Allows the user to modify the size of the window.
width	Initial window width, in pixels.
height	Initial window height, in pixels.

Related Items

See the document and frame objects.

See the defaultStatus, frames, parent, self, status, top, and window properties.

See the alert, close, confirm, open, prompt, setTimeout, and clearTimeout methods.

See the onLoad and onUnload event handlers.

Fig. QR.11 Some of the various features of a Navigator window that are controlled through the window.open method.

Menu bar   Tool bar   Directories

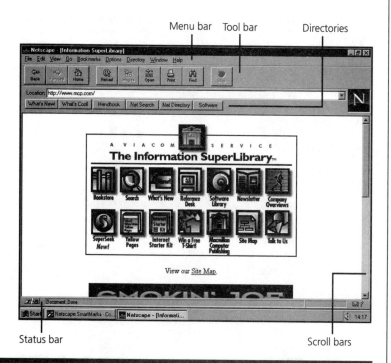

Status bar   Scroll bars

window

(Property)

A synonym for the current window.

```
frameName.window
[windowName.]window
```

Usage

The window property is used to remove ambiguity between a window and form object of the same name. Although window also applies to the current frame, it is less ambiguous to use the self property.

Related Items

Property of frame and window.

See self property.

write

(Method)

Writes one or more lines to a document window.

```
document.write(string)
```

Usage

Strings written to a window can include HTML tags and JavaScript expressions, including numeric, string, and logical values. The write method does not add a new line (
 or /n) character to the end of the output. If write is called from an event handler, the current document is cleared if a new window is not created for the output.

Related Items

Method of document.

See the close, clear, open, and writeln methods.

writeln

(Method)

Writes one or more lines to a document window, followed by a newline character.

```
document.writeln(string)
```

Usage

Like its cousin write, writeln can include HTML tags and JavaScript expressions, including numeric, string, and logical values. If writln is called from an event handler, the current document is cleared if a new window is not created for the output.

HTML ignores the newline character, unless it is used within <PRE> tags.

Related Items

Method of document.

See the close, clear, open, and write methods.

JAVASCRIPT STATEMENTS

The statements used to control program flow in JavaScript are similar to Java and C. A statement can span several lines if needed or several statements can be placed on the same line.

There are a couple of important items to remember. First, blocks of statements, such as a function defintion, must be enclosed in curly braces. This is how JavaScript delineates blocks of code. Second, a semicolon must be placed between all statements. Without a semicolon, script behavior is unpredictable.

Since JavaScript is not strict in its formatting, you must provide the line breaks and indentation to make sure the code is readable and easy to understand later.

break

Terminates the current `for` or `while` loop and passes control to the first statement after the loop.

Usage

The following example adds elements on a form, assuming that all the elements contain numeric values. If a 0 is encountered, the adding stops.

```
function checkValues(form) {
      var total
      for (I=0; I<=form.elements.length; I++) {
        if (element[I].value = "0") {
             break; }
        else {
```

```
                    total += I;
                    document.write("The running total
is "+total); }
    }
    return total
}
```

comment

Notes from the script author that are ignored by the interpreter. Single line comments are preceded by //. Multiple line comments begin with /* and end with */.

Usage

```
/* These comments could start here
and
end
down here. */
...statements...
// This comment is limited to this line only.
```

continue

Passes control to the condition in a while loop and to the update expression in a for loop. The important difference from break is that the loop is not terminated.

Usage

The following example adds elements on a form, assuming that all the elements contain numeric values. If a value less than 0 is encountered, it is not included in the running total.

```
function checkValues(form) {
        var total
        for (I=0; I<=form.elements.length; I++) {
           if (element[I].value < 0) {
                continue; }
```

```
        else {
              total += I;
              document.write("The running total
is "+total); }
    }
    return total

}
```

for

Creates a loop with three optional expressions enclosed in parentheses and separated by semicolons, followed by a set of statements to be executed during the loop:

```
for (initialExpression; condition;
updateExpression) {
        ...statements...
}
```

The `initial` expression is used to initialize the counter variable, which can be a new variable declared with `var`.

The `condition` expression is evaluated on each pass through the loop. If the condition is `true`, the loop statements are executed. If the condition is omitted, then it defaults to `true`, and the loop continues until an error or `break` is reached.

The `update` expression is used to increment the counter variable. It is also optional and can be updated programatically within the loop statements.

Usage

`for` creates a loop that continues until an error occurs or a `break` statement is executed. The `increment` variable is increased by 2 each time through the loop.

```
for (var increment=0; ; increment+=2) {
        ...statements...
}
```

The following example is a loop that does not update its counter. If the counter is never updated in the course of the statements, then the value will remain 10.

```
for (var increment=10; increment<101; ) {
        ...statements...
}
```

for...in

Iterates a variable for all of properties of an object. For each property, for...in executes the statement block:

```
for (objectVariable) {
...statements...
}
```

Usage

for...in is a useful function for debugging because of its ability to display all of the properties of an object in one loop.

```
function objectDisplay (obj) {
    var displayLine;
    for (var prop in obj) {
            displayLine = obj.name + "." + prop + " =
" + obj[prop];
            document.write(displayLine + "<BR>")
    }
    document.write("End of object " + obj.name)
}
```

function

Declares a JavaScript function with a name and parameters. To return a value, the function must include a return statement. A function definition cannot be nested within another function.

```
function name ([parameter [...,parameter]]) {
        ...statements...
}
```

if...else

A conditional statement that executes the first set of statements if the condition is `true` and the statements following `else` if `false`. `if...else` statements can be nested to any level. If single statements are used after the statements, curly braces are not needed.

```
if (condition) {
        ...statements...
} [else {
        ...statements...
}]
```

Usage

The following example converts minutes to a two-digit number for use in a clock display.

```
function makeMinutes() {
        var minString = "";
        var now = new Date();
        var min = Date.getMinutes();
        if (min < 10) {
           minString += ":0" + min; }
        else {
           minString += ":" + min; }
        return minString
}
```

return

Specifies a value to be returned by a function.

```
return expression;
```

Usage

The following example takes three strings and puts them together, separated by commas.

```
function stringAssemble (string1, string2, string3)
{
        return string1 + ", " + string2 + ", " +
string3
}
```

var

Declares a variable and optionally initializes it to a value. The scope of a variable is the current function or—when declared outside a function—the current document.

```
var variableName [=value] [..., variableName
[=value]]
```

Usage

The `globalString` variable can be used in any function or script in the current document, whereas the variable `localString` can only be used within the `bracket` function.

```
var globalString
function bracket() {
        var localString = "[" + globalString + "]";
        document.write(localString);
}
```

while

Repeats a loop while an expression is `true`. If the condition is no longer true, execution drops to the first statement after the `while` statements.

```
while (condition) {
        ...statements...
}
```

Usage

The following example examines a string for a specific character and stops its search when it finds it or runs out of characters to look for.

```
var found = false
n = 0
while (n <= searchString.length || !found) {
        if (searchString.charAt[n] == "?")
          found = true
        else
          n++;
}
```

with

Establishes a default object for a set of statements. Any property references without an object are assumed to use the default object.

```
with (object) {
statements…
}
```

Usage

The with statement is especially useful when applied to the Math object for a set of calculations. For example:

```
with (Math) {
var Value1 = cos(angle);
var Value2 = sin(angle);
}
```

replaces:

```
var Value1 = Math.cos(angle);
var Value2 = Math.sin(angle);
```

OPERATORS

The two types of operations in JavaScript are those that assign a value to a variable and those that create a value without an assignment.

The expression

```
x = 1 + 1
```

has two parts. First, the expression on the right is evaluated, resulting in 2. Then, the result is assigned to the variable on the left, **x**. On the other hand

```
1 + 1
```

evaluates to 2. The expression is completed but since there is no assignment operator, no assignment is made. When the rest of the expression such as a method or function call is completed, the value is abandoned.

JavaScript includes a `null` value for variables that have not been assigned another value. Any attempt to use a `null` variable in an equation results in an error, unless it is an assignment for initializing a variable, such as `timerID = null`.

Special Operators

```
.    //call
[]   //index
()   //member
```

The period is used to separate objects from their properties and methods.

Brackets are used for denoting indexes in arrays, such as `form` and `elements`.

Special Operators

Parentheses have two uses. First, they contain the parameters and arguments for functions and methods. Second, they are used to give order to complex equations. Although the following two equations appear to be the same, the results are different.

```
I = 5 * 5 + 10    //Result: 35
I = 5 * (5 + 10)  //Result: 75
```

Usage

When processing an equation, JavaScript begins with any operators inside parentheses and works its way out until all operations are completed. For the first example, the multiplication symbol has higher precedence than the addition symbol, so JavaScript multiplies 5 times 5 and then adds 10. In the second example, the parentheses force the computation of 5 plus 10 and the result is multiplied times 5.

Unary Operators

```
++  //increment
-   //decrement
!   //complement
-   //unary negation
```

The double-plus and double-minus are used to increment or decrement single variables and can be used prefix or postfix.

Usage

When the double operator is placed in front of the variable (prefix), the operation is completed before the assignment is made. When the double operator is placed after the variable (postfix), the assignment is made to the variable on the left and then the operation is completed.

```
J = 1
I = J++  //I=1, J=2
I = ++J  //I=3, J=3
```

The complement operator is used for Boolean values to reverse the value although the variable itself is not changed.

```
testResult = true
document.write(testResult)   //"true"
document.write(!testResult)  //"false"
```

Unary negation changes the sign of the variable, just as multiplying the number times -1 does.

Binary Operators

```
+   //addition
-   //subtraction
*   //multiplication
/   //division
%   //modulus
```

Binary operators need two operands. Addition, subtraction, multiplication, and division are the standard versions of these operators.

Usage

Modulus is a special division operator that only returns the remainder of the operation. For example:.

```
I2 = 8 % 2  //returns 0
I3 = 8 % 3  //returns 2
```

Bitwise Operators

```
~   //bitwise complement
<<  //left shift
>>  //right shift
>>> //right shift with zero fill
&   //and
^   //xor
|   //or
```

Bitwise operators work on variables at their lowest level: bits (0 and 1). Shift operators convert the operand on the left to a 32-bit integer, which is shifted by the number of bits specified on the right side. The logical bitwise operators convert both values to 32-bit integers before comparing them.

Usage

Bitwise complements are similar to the regular complement, only at the bit level. All bits with a 1 are changed to 0 and a 0 is changed to 1.

Left shift moves all bits to the left by the number of places on the right side of the equation filling in with zeroes behind, whereas the zero-fill right shift works in the same way in the opposite direction. The standard right shift propagates the leftmost bit.

```
function bitShift() {
        I = -1
        for (increment = 0; increment<9;
    ➡increment++) {document.write(I)
          I = I << 1
        }
}
```

The bitwise logical operators work in a slightly different way. When compared with another value, they return a value based on a bit-by-bit comparison based on Tables 4.7, 4.8 and 4.9.

Table 4.7 Boolean Operations — And (&)

Bit1	Bit2	Result
1	1	1
0	1	0
1	0	0
0	0	0

Table 4.8 Boolean Operations — Xor (^)

Bit1	Bit2	Result
1	1	0
0	1	1
1	0	1
0	0	0

Table 4.9	Boolean Operations — Or (/)	
Bit1	Bit2	Result
1	1	1
0	1	1
1	0	1
0	0	0

For example, the 4-bit binary value of 13 is represented as 1101. The results of binary operations with 15 (binary 1111) and 0 (binary 0000) would be return the following values:

```
bin13 = 13; //1101
bin15 = 15; //1111
bin0 = 0; //0000
document.writeln(bin13 & bin15); //results in 13
(1101)
document.writeln(bin13 & bin0); //results in 0
(0000)
document.writeln(bin13 ^ bin15); //results in 2
(0010)
document.writeln(bin13 ^ bin0); //results in 13
(1101)
document.writeln(bin13 | bin15); //results in 15
(1111)
document.writeln(bin13 | bin0); //results in 13
(1101)
```

Relational/Equality

```
<   //less than
>   //greater than
<=  //less than or equal to
>=  //greater than or equal to
==  //equal to
!=  //not equal to
?:  //conditional
```

Relational/Equality

A Boolean value is returned when using variables or literals with the relational/equality operators.

Usage

It is important to note the last two operators in the example above: equal and not-equal.

A double-equal is needed so JavaScript doesn't confuse the comparison for an assignment. For not-equal, a common convention is opposing arrows (<>). In JavaScript, however, the implementation is formed by adding the complement operator.

The conditional operation is a special type of comparison that is only used with the assignment operator. It functions as an if-then statement for assigning a value.

```
underAge = (age=>21) ? "no" : "yes"
```

If the expression in the parentheses evaluates to true, then the first value is assigned to the variable. If it evaluates to false, the value after the colon is assigned.

Logical

```
&& //and
|| //or
```

The logical operators are for comparing two Boolean values, typically other relational/equality expressions.

Usage

The logical operators work in the same manner as the bitwise and and or, only at the variable level.

In the following example, if the variable age is greater than or equal to 21 and the variable hasID is a Boolean true, then the block of statements will be executed.

```
if ( (age>=21) && (hasID) ) {
    ...statements...
}
```

Logical comparisons short-circuit before completing the right half of the expression, depending on the comparison being made.

```
false && anyExpression   //Shorts to false
true || anyExpression    //Shorts to true
```

Assignment

```
=   //assign
+=  //addition, concatenate
-=  //subtraction
*=  //multiplication
/=  //division
%=  //modulus
<<= //bitwise left shift
>>= //bitwise right shift
>>>=//bitwise zero fill right shift
&=  //bitwise and
^=  //bitwise xor
|=  //bitwise or
```

When combined with one of the other binary operators, the assignment operator offers a convenient shorthand for updating variables.

Usage

For example, the following two statements do the same task (adding 5 to the variable `shipping`):

```
shipping = shipping + 5;
shipping += 5;
```

The `+=` operator can also be used to concatenate strings.

```
sentence = "";
subject = "The dog";
predicate = "walked home.";
sentence += subject;
sentence += predicate;
document.write(sentence);  //results in "The dog
walked home."
```

Operator Precedence

Precedence refers to the order in which compound operations are computed. Operators on the same level have equal precedence. Calculations are computed from left to right on all binary operations, beginning with the operators at the top of the list and working down.

call, member	.	[]	()	
negation/increment	++	—	!	~ —
multiply/divide	*	/	%	
addition/subtraction	+	—		
bitwise shift	<<	>>	>>>	
relational	<	>	<=	>=
equality	==	!=		
bitwise-and	&			
bitwise-xor	^			
bitwise-or	|			
logical-and	&&			
logical-or	||			
conditional	?:			
assignment	=	+= -= *= /= %= <<= >>= >>>= &= ^= |=		
comma	,			

REFERENCE TABLES

ISO Latin Character Set

When using methods such as `escape` and `unescape`, the returned values relate to the ISO Latin character set. In Table QR.10, you can see a listing of the values and characters for this set.

Table QR.10   ISO Latin Characters

Decimal Value	Character	Entity Reference
0	NUL	
1	SOH	
2	STX	
3	ETX	
4	EOT	
5	ENQ	
6	ACK	
7	BEL	
8	BS	
9	HT	
10	NL	
11	VT	
12	NP	

continues

ISO Latin Character Set

Decimal Value	Character	Entity Reference
13	CR	
14	SO	
15	SI	
16	DLE	
17	DC1	
18	DC2	
19	DC3	
20	DC4	
21	NAK	
22	SYN	
23	ETB	
24	CAN	
25	EM	
26	SUB	
27	ESC	
28	FS	
29	GS	
30	RS	
31	US	
32	SP	
33	!	
34	"	&quot;
35	#	
36	$	
37	%	
38	&	&amp

ISO Latin Character Set

Decimal Value	Character	Entity Reference
39	'	
40	(	
41	)	
42	*	
43	+	
44	,	
45	-	
46	.	
47	/	
48	0	
49	1	
50	2	
51	3	
52	4	
53	5	
54	6	
55	7	
56	8	
57	9	
58	:	
59	;	
60	<	&lt
61	=	
62	>	&gt
63	?	
64	@	
65	A	

continues

ISO Latin Character Set

Table QR.10 Continued

Decimal Value	Character	Entity Reference
66	B	
67	C	
68	D	
69	E	
70	F	
71	G	
72	H	
73	I	
74	J	
75	K	
76	L	
77	M	
78	N	
79	O	
80	P	
81	Q	
82	R	
83	S	
84	T	
85	U	
86	V	
87	W	
88	X	
89	Y	
90	Z	
91	[	

ISO Latin Character Set

Decimal Value	Character	Entity Reference
92	\	
93	]	
94	^	
95	_	
96	'	
97	a	
98	b	
99	c	
100	d	
101	e	
102	f	
103	g	
104	h	
105	i	
106	j	
107	k	
108	l	
109	m	
110	n	
111	o	
112	p	
113	q	
114	r	
115	s	
116	t	
117	u	
118	v	

continues

ISO Latin Character Set

Table QR.10   Continued

Decimal Value	Character	Entity Reference
119	w	
120	x	
121	y	
122	z	
123	{	
124			
125	}	
126	~	
127	DEL	
128–159	—	
160		
161	¡	
162	¢	
163	£	
164	¤	
165	¥	
166			
167	§	
168	¨	
169	©	
170	ª	
171	«	
172	¬	
173	–	
174	®	
175	¯	

ISO Latin Character Set

Decimal Value	Character	Entity Reference
176	°	
177	±	
178	²	
179	³	
180	´	
181	µ	
182	¶	
183	·	
184	¸	
185	¹	
186	º	
187	»	
188	–	
189	–	
190	–	
191	¿	
192	À	&Agrave;
193	Á	&Aacute;
194	Â	&Acirc;
195	Ã	&Atilde;
196	Ä	&Auml;
197	Å	&Aring;
198	Æ	&AElig;
199	Ç	&Ccedil;
200	È	&Egrave;
201	É	&Eacute;
202	Ê	&Ecirc;

continues

ISO Latin Character Set

Table QR.10   Continued

Decimal Value	Character	Entity Reference
203	Ë	&Euml;
204	Ì	&Igrave;
205	Í	&Iacute;
206	Î	&Icirc;
207	Ï	&Iuml;
208	–	
209	Ñ	&Ntilde;
210	Ò	&Ograve;
211	Ó	&Oacute;
212	Ô	&Ocirc;
213	Õ	&Otilde;
214	Ö	&Ouml;
215	×	
216	Ø	&Oslash;
217	Ù	&Ugrave;
218	Ú	&Uacute;
219	Û	&Ucirc;
220	Ü	&Uuml;
221	Y	&Yacute;
222	–	&THORN;
223	ß	&szlig;
224	à	&agrave;
225	á	&aacute;
226	â	&acirc;
227	ã	&atilde;
228	ä	&auml;

ISO Latin Character Set

Decimal Value	Character	Entity Reference
229	å	&aring;
230	æ	&aelig;
231	ç	&ccedil;
232	è	&egrave;
233	é	&eacute;
234	ê	&ecirc;
235	ë	&euml;
236	ì	&igrave;
237	í	&iacute;
238	î	&icirc;
239	ï	&iuml;
240		&eth;
241	ñ	&ntilde;
242	ò	&ograve;
243	ó	&oacute;
244	ô	&ocirc;
245	õ	&otilde;
246	ö	&ouml;
247	÷	
248	ø	&oslash;
249	ù	&ugrave;
250	ú	&uacute;
251	û	&ucirc;
252	ü	&uuml;
253	y	&yacute;
254	_	&thorn;
255	ÿ	&yuml;

Color Values

Colors can be referenced in a variety of properties in two ways. The first is by using the string literal, which is the color's name. The second is by using an RGB hexadecimal triplet formed by combining the three color values. For example, a specific shade of blue is represented by the string literal `aliceblue` and the triplet F0F8FF. The actual color displayed by the browser is determined by the range of colors supported by the client machine—a VGA monitor with 16 colors is going to be much less dramatic than an SVGA with 16 million.

Color/String Literal	Red	Green	Blue
aliceblue	F0	F8	FF
antiquewhite	FA	EB	D7
aqua	00	FF	FF
aquamarine	7F	FF	D4
azure	F0	FF	FF
beige	F5	F5	DC
bisque	FF	E4	C4
black	00	00	00
blanchedalmond	FF	EB	CD
blue	00	00	FF
blueviolet	8A	2B	E2
brown	A5	2A	2A
burlywood	DE	B8	87
cadetblue	5F	9E	A0
chartreuse	7F	FF	00
chocolate	D2	69	1E
coral	FF	7F	50
cornflowerblue	64	95	ED
cornsilk	FF	F8	DC
crimson	DC	14	3C
cyan	00	FF	FF
darkblue	00	00	8B
darkcyan	00	8B	8B

Color Values

Color/String Literal	Red	Green	Blue
darkgoldenrod	B8	86	0B
darkgray	A9	A9	A9
darkgreen	00	64	00
darkkhaki	BD	B7	6B
darkmagenta	8B	00	8B
darkolivegreen	55	6B	2F
darkorange	FF	8C	00
darkorchid	99	32	CC
darkred	8B	00	00
darksalmon	E9	96	7A
darkseagreen	8F	BC	8F
darkslateblue	48	3D	8B
darkslategray	2F	4F	4F
darkturquoise	00	CE	D1
darkviolet	94	00	D3
deeppink	FF	14	93
deepskyblue	00	BF	FF
dimgray	69	69	69
dodgerblue	1E	90	FF
firebrick	B2	22	22
floralwhite	FF	FA	F0
forestgreen	22	8B	22
fuchsia	FF	00	FF
gainsboro	DC	DC	DC
ghostwhite	F8	F8	FF
gold	FF	D7	00
goldenrod	DA	A5	20
gray	80	80	80
green	00	80	00
greenyellow	AD	FF	2F

continues

Color Values

continued

Color/String Literal	Red	Green	Blue
honeydew	F0	FF	F0
hotpink	FF	69	B4
indianred	CD	5C	5C
indigo	4B	00	82
ivory	FF	FF	F0
khaki	F0	E6	8C
lavender	E6	E6	FA
lavenderblush	FF	F0	F5
lawngreen	7C	FC	00
lemonchiffon	FF	FA	CD
lightblue	AD	D8	E6
lightcoral	F0	80	80
lightcyan	E0	FF	FF
lightgoldenrodyellow	FA	FA	D2
lightgreen	90	EE	90
lightgrey	D3	D3	D3
lightpink	FF	B6	C1
lightsalmon	FF	A0	7A
lightseagreen	20	B2	AA
lightskyblue	87	CE	FA
lightslategray	77	88	99
lightsteelblue	B0	C4	DE
lightyellow	FF	FF	E0
lime	00	FF	00
limegreen	32	CD	32
linen	FA	F0	E6
magenta	FF	00	FF
maroon	80	00	00
mediumaquamarine	66	CD	AA
mediumblue	00	00	CD
mediumorchid	BA	55	D3

Color Values

Color/String Literal	Red	Green	Blue
mediumpurple	93	70	DB
mediumseagreen	3C	B3	71
mediumslateblue	7B	68	EE
mediumspringgreen	00	FA	9A
mediumturquoise	48	D1	CC
mediumvioletred	C7	15	85
midnightblue	19	19	70
mintcream	F5	FF	FA
mistyrose	FF	E4	E1
moccasin	FF	E4	B5
navajowhite	FF	DE	AD
navy	00	00	80
oldlace	FD	F5	E6
olive	80	80	00
olivedrab	6B	8E	23
orange	FF	A5	00
orangered	FF	45	00
orchid	DA	70	D6
palegoldenrod	EE	E8	AA
palegreen	98	FB	98
paleturquoise	AF	EE	EE
palevioletred	DB	70	93
papayawhip	FF	EF	D5
peachpuff	FF	DA	B9
peru	CD	85	3F
pink	FF	C0	CB
plum	DD	A0	DD
powderblue	B0	E0	E6
purple	80	00	80
red	FF	00	00
rosybrown	BC	8F	8F

continues

Color Values

continued

royalblue	41	69	E1
saddlebrown	8B	45	13
salmon	FA	80	72
sandybrown	F4	A4	60
seagreen	2E	8B	57
seashell	FF	F5	EE
sienna	A0	52	2D
silver	C0	C0	C0
skyblue	87	CE	EB
slateblue	6A	5A	CD
slategray	70	80	90
snow	FF	FA	FA
springgreen	00	FF	7F
steelblue	46	82	B4
tan	D2	B4	8C
teal	00	80	80
thistle	D8	BF	D8
tomato	FF	63	47
turquoise	40	E0	D0
violet	EE	82	EE
wheat	F5	DE	B3
white	FF	FF	FF
whitesmoke	F5	F5	F5
yellow	FF	FF	00
yellowgreen	9A	CD	32

Reserved Words

The following words cannot be used as user objects or variables in coding JavaScript. Not all are currently in use by JavaScript—they are reserved for future use.

Reserved Words

abstract	float	public
boolean	for	return
break	function	short
byte	goto	static
case	if	super
catch	implements	switch
char	import	synchronized
class	in	this
const	instanceof	throw
continue	int	throws
default	interface	transient
do	long	true
double	native	try
else	new	var
extends	null	void
false	package	while
final	private	with
finally	protected	

TASK REFERENCE

JavaScript provides tools to perform a variety of tasks in an HTML document without the need to interact with the server.

New Browser

One of the powerful features of JavaScript that makes it useful for implementing demonstrations and tours is its ability to spawn new versions of the client browser with controllable levels of functionality.

The basic command to create a new browser is:

```
windowVar = window.open("URL", "windowName"
[, "windowFeatures"])
```

To open a plain window with hotlink-only navigation:

```
//Note: Setting one feature automatically sets all
non-mentioned features to false.
window.open("URL", "windowName", "toolbar=no")
```

To open a window without the directories or menubar:

```
window.open("URL", "windowName",
"toolbar=yes,location=yes,directories=no,status=yes,
menubar=no,scrollbars=yes,resizable=yes")
```

For more information see:

> window object
>
> open method

Creating a Custom-Navigation Web Site

One of the powerful capabilities of JavaScript is its ability to control the functionality of the browser (see "Task Reference, New Browser"). This is useful for creating guided-tour or demonstration programs. To create a site requires a front door that generates the rest of the application.

```
<FORM>
<INPUT TYPE="button" NAME="tour" VALUE="Start Tour"

onClick="window.open('tourframes.html','tourWindow',
'toolbar=no')">
</FORM>
```

The `tourframes.html` file creates the frames containing a starting page and navigation bar.

```
<FRAMESET COLS="%10,%90">
    <FRAME SRC="navbar.html">
    <FRAME SRC="tourstart.html" NAME="contentWin">
</FRAMESET>
```

The `navBar` file is a simple set of buttons with custom `onClick` event handlers to direct the browser.

```
<FORM NAME = "navBar">
<INPUT TYPE="button" NAME="back" VALUE="  <-- Back
"onClick="contentWin.document.history.back()">
<INPUT TYPE="button" NAME="forw" VALUE="Forward -->
"onClick="contentWin.document.history.forward()">
<INPUT TYPE="button" NAME="home" VALUE="Home"
onClick="contentWin.document.history.go(0)">
<INPUT TYPE="button" NAME="quit" VALUE="Quit the
Tour" onClick="parent.close()">
</FORM>
```

To prevent premature escapes, the quit button could also call a function that confirms the user's choice before closing the window.

For more information, see:

> `button`, `document`, `form`, `history`, and `window` objects
>
> `back`, `close`, `forward`, and `go` methods
>
> `top` and `parent` properties
>
> `onClick` event handler

Self-Resetting Status Messages

A sometimes annoying side effect of the `window.status` property is its persistence. Once set, it doesn't change unless another `window.status` assignment is encountered.

You can overcome this attribute using the `setTimeout` method.

```
timeDelay = 1500 //1.5 seconds

function eraseStatus () {
      window.status = "" //This can also be set to
a 'default' message.
};

function setStatus (statusText) {
      window.status = statusText;
      setTimeout("eraseStatus()",timeDelay)
}
```

Using these two functions is a simple matter of including the `setStatus` function in the `onMouseOver` event.

```
<A HREF=URL onMouseOver="setStatus('Your message
here.'); return true">linkText</A>
```

For more information see:

> `window` object
>
> `status` property
>
> `setTimeout` method
>
> `onMouseOver` event handler

Platform-Specific Newline Characters

Which version of the newline character to use depends on the platform used by the client. Windows needs an `/r` in addition to the `/n` needed for all other platforms. Because it's impossible to control which platforms access your page, a simple function can ensure that the proper form of the newline character is used.

```
function brk() {
        if (navigator.appVersion.lastIndexOf('Win')
!= -1)
            return "\r\n"
    else
            return "\n"
}
```

For more information see:

> `navigator` object
>
> `appVersion` property
>
> `lastIndexOf` method

Validating Form Information

Validating information through CGI scripts is a time-consuming process. Not only is there the added communication between the client and server, but time and expertise are also needed to develop the actual CGI script.

Including form validation with JavaScript directly on the HTML page increases the speed and localizes the process to the end user. This makes it much harder for end users to send incompatible data that could cause damage to the server.

There are several ways to do form validation but a basic tenet is adding a JavaScript function to a true submit button. The HTML definition of the submit button could look like this:

```
<INPUT TYPE="BUTTON" NAME="SUBMIT" VALUE="SUBMIT"
onClick="checkInformation(this.form)">
```

`checkInformation` provides for verifying that the information meets CGI script expectations. If not, it should at least return to the document without submitting or return focus to the offending items. If everything passes muster, then the function can also submit the form.

```
function checkInformation(form) {
        ...validation statements ...;
        if (validationPassed) {
          form.submit(); }
        return;
}
```

For more information see:

form and button objects

focus methods

onClick event handlers

Creating Arrays

Although JavaScript uses arrays for several of its objects (forms, elements, etc.), it doesn't provide a straightforward method to create user-defined arrays—one of the staples of data processing.

Here is a function to create a new array by initializing the elements. This is useful for small arrays but is unwieldy for larger implementations.

```
function arrayCreator() {
        this.length = initArray.arguments.length; //
counts the number of arguments included when the
function is called
        for (var I=0; I<this.length; I==) {
          this[I+1] = userArray.arguments[I] //load
the new values into the array
    }
}
```

To initialize a new array, use the function with this syntax:

```
var arrayName = new userArray(argument1
[,argument2] [,argument3] [etc.])
```

Generating a Random Number (Non-UNIX)

At present, the random method works only with UNIX versions of Netscape. There is another way of generating pseudo-random numbers without using the built-in method. This is called a *calculated random number* and if accessed repeatedly over a short time, reveals its biases and true nonrandom nature.

Generating a Random Number (Non-UNIX)

To ensure compatibility for a script across platforms, any script depending on random numbers should not use the `random` method and instead should rely on a user-defined function like the one below.

```
function UnixMachine() {
        if (navigator.appVersion.lastIndexOf('Unix')
!= -1)
           return true
        else
           return false
}

function randomNumber() {
        if (UnixMachine()) {
           num = Math.random() }
        else {
           num = Math.abs(Math.sin(Date.getTime()));
}
        return num;
}
```

This generates a number between 0 and 1, and works well for applications needing random numbers every few seconds. If random numbers are needed with greater frequency, you need to add more variation into the equation, such as a different computation (`cos`, `tan`, `log`) every third division of time or something similar.

For more information see:

`Date` and `Math` objects

`random` method

`function` and `return` statements

INTERNET RESOURCES

B ecause of JavaScript's very specific platform base (it's currently recognized only by Netscape Navigator), the number of "official" online resources that directly address it are few and far between. However, the "unofficial" resources (put up by experimental souls who wish to share their discoveries in this new technology) are growing at a rapid rate.

The World Wide Web

Since JavaScript is *for* the Web, it's only appropriate that the best sources of information on its use are found *on* the Web. As with most other Internet-based sources, the bulk of JavaScript sites are primarily Java-oriented, with JavaScript covered as a subsection.

The following list is by no means comprehensive. To keep up on new offerings on the Web, your best bet is to take advantage of the Other Hot Links pages that many of the sites have.

Navigator was the first browser that supported JavaScript, making Netscape's home site a good place to check periodically, especially for updates/additions to the JavaScript language specification.

Netscape also has its own Development Partners Program, providing subscribers with extended technical and programming support, information on upcoming products, extensions, plug-ins, access to pre-beta releases of new browsers, servers, and plug-ins.

Also be sure to check out the Netscape ColorCenter at **http://www.hidaho.com/colorcenter/**. This is a handy place to compare the values of colors against their appearance on the screen.

Voodoo JavaScript Tutorial (http://rummelplatz.uni-mannheim.de/~skoch/js/script.htm)

Voodoo JavaScript Tutorial is a continuing tutorial presented in easy-to-digest sections covering the basics of JavaScript. It includes examples built in to the page, along with descriptive text and code examples. It's a good place to get your feet wet.

The Unofficial JavaScript Resource Center (http://www.intercom.net/user/mecha/java/index.html)

The Unofficial JavaScript Resource Center is a new, well-produced site devoted to JavaScript. At first, it was fairly limited but it promises to grow with more examples and techniques for a range of users.

The idea is to provide a few examples and snippets of code to copy and drop into place. Its organization will make it a useful resource as the content expands.

Danny Goodman's JavaScript Pages (http://www/dannyg.com:80/javascript)

Danny Goodman's JavaScript Pages are a collection of examples covering more advanced concepts in JavaScript, including cookies. Danny Goodman is one of the de facto experts on JavaScript on the Web, and he gives some good examples for learning and adapting other applications.

JavaScript Index (http://www.c2.org/~andreww/javascript/)

JavaScript Index is a solid compendium of JavaScript implementations and experimentations, including a growing list of personal home pages that show off a variety of JavaScript tricks. A subset of the site is the **JavaScript Library**, a small but expanding collection of source code from around the Web community.

Gamelan (http://www.gamelan.com/)

Called *The* On-Line Java Index, EarthWeb's Gamelan has an extensive collection of links to other sites, examples, tools, utilities, and other interesting things. Although primarily targeting Java, the JavaScript section is quite sizable as well.

Sun Microsystems (http://java.sun.com/)

At Sun Microsystems, the place where it *all* started, Sun hosts the Java home site. Additionally, Sun maintains the Java Users Group (a subgroup inside the Sun Users Group) and several mailing and notification lists to keep developers informed of the latest events.

JavaWorld (http://www.javaworld.com/)

To support its efforts to integrate Java development into Latte, Borland's host site for Java development promises to keep Java developers informed.

Symantec (http://cafe.symantec.com/)

Symantec led the pack when it came to providing a development platform for Java applet creation for Windows and Macintosh. With the first publicly available (for free and for Windows NT/95) Java development add-on to their popular C++ package, Symantec provided the first graphical user interface (GUI)-based development environment for applet creation.

Dimension X (http://www.dnx.com/)

Dimension X is the home of Liquid Reality, a Java applet development platform that merges the capabilities of a 3-D modeling package with a Java applet builder.

The Java Developer (http://www.digitalfocus.com/faq/)

Sponsored by Digital Focus, the Java Developer serves as the home site for The Java Developer FAQ. It is one of the more interesting implementations of frames to present search and question submission buttons as you browse the site.

Usenet

Several Usenet newsgroups have sprung up to provide channels for developers looking for guidance with Java, JavaScript, and Web programming in general. These are as follows:

comp.lang.javascript

comp.lang.javascript is dedicated to JavaScript development. A large number of messages are posted to this forum every day, including many from the established gurus of JavaScript. It contains a lot of information if you take the time to peruse all the messages.

netscape.navigator (news:// secnews.netscape.com)

It never hurts to have a direct line monitored by the folks who developed JavaScript at Netscape, and netscape.navigator is the closest thing there is. JavaScript topics are definitely in the minority in this group but they're there if you look.

Note the different news server. The title implies it's secure, but it seems to be readily available for browsing and posting.

comp.lang.java

comp.lang.java is the group from which the comp.lang.javascript group sprang. It deals specifically with Sun's Java language but occasionally has information about JavaScript also.

comp.infosystems.www.authoring.*

The traditional collection of newsgroups for Web-oriented discussion has been comp.infosystems.www. As the Web has expanded, so have they, covering everything from browsers to announcements of newly opened Web sites.

Although there is no JavaScript-specific group in the comp.infosystems heirarchy, there are several that cover the various facets of Web authoring:

- comp.infosystems.www.authoring.cgi
- comp.infosystems.www.authoring.html

- **comp.infosystems.www.authoring.images**
- **comp.infosystems.www.authoring.misc**

Mailing Lists

For those who prefer the thrill of receiving e-mail until their inboxes burst, there are mailing lists dedicated to JavaScript that offer similar information to the Usenet newsgroups.

Keep in mind, however, that mailing lists are a lot like a telephone party line and can get rather chatty (the downside being that you have to wade through all the flotsam in your inbox to figure out what you can use).

If you plan to use mailing lists heavily, you might want to look into an e-mail program that enables *threading* or linking together messages that share the same subject to help keep the volume organized.

A word about mailing lists. Although you post your questions and comments to the list's address (for rebroadcast to the rest of the list's readers), subscribing to and unsubscribing from the list are done through *a separate e-mail address*, specifically the address of the *listserver*.

The following lists mention both the list address and the listserver address, and sending subscribe requests to the list address (so everyone on the list knows you don't know what you're doing) is a guaranteed way to get branded a "newbie."

If you want more information on how to communicate with the listserver (or on other possible lists of a particular server), you can send a message to the listserver address with `help` in the message body.

javascript@obscure.org

Sponsored by the Obscure Organization (http://www.obscure.org/) and TeleGlobal Media, Inc. (http://www.tgm.com/), the JavaScript Index is the only mailing list dedicated specifically to JavaScript.

The discussion gets pretty varied and ranges from introductory questions to more involved discussions on how best to handle animations, framing, reloads, and so on.

To subscribe, send a message to `majordomo@obscure.org` with `subscribe javascript` in the message body. Alternatively, you can point your browser at `http://www.obscure.org/javascript/` for further information.

java@borland.com

A companion newsletter that parallels the activity on Borland's JavaWorld site, the Borland Java newsletter keeps you informed about Borland's work on integrating Java technology into their development tools. To subscribe, send a message to `listserv@borland.com` with `subscribe java {your first name} {your last name}` in the message body.

java-announce@java.sun.com

Sun Microsystems, the home of Java, has its own collection of mailing lists. The `java-announce` list is primarily for notifications of new Java-related tools. To subscribe, send a message to `majordomo@java.sun.com` with `subscribe java-announce` in the message body.

INDEX

big method

equations

statements

window object